WALKS INTO HISTORY
NORFOLK & SUFFOLK

John Wilks

COUNTRYSIDE BOOKS
NEWBURY BERKSHIRE

Contents

AREA MAP SHOWING LOCATION OF THE WALKS

PUBLISHER'S NOTE

We hope that you obtain considerable enjoyment from this book; great care has been taken in its preparation. Although at the time of publication all routes followed public rights of way or permitted paths, diversion orders can be made and permissions withdrawn.

We cannot, of course, be held responsible for such diversion orders and any inaccuracies in the text which result from these or any other changes to the routes nor any damage which might result from walkers trespassing on private property. We are anxious though that all details covering the walks are kept up to date and would therefore welcome information from readers which would be relevant to future editions.

The simple sketch maps that accompany the walks in this book are based on notes made by the author whilst checking out the routes on the ground. However, for the benefit of a proper map, we do recommend that you purchase the relevant Ordnance Survey map. These are widely available, especially through booksellers and local newsagents.

INTRODUCTION

History is all around you no matter where you walk in Suffolk and Norfolk. The wide open skies, generally level terrain and sheer variety of landscape in East Anglia make walking here a year-round delight, and the information that accompanies the walks in this book explains so much that we might otherwise miss.

The Norfolk Brecklands, for instance, with their open, sandy heaths, are ideal for an enjoyable few hours' walking, but to discover that at Grimes Graves you are walking where our ancestors lived, worked and worshipped over 5,000 years ago adds so much more to the experience. Or perhaps you will take the route along the sea wall by the Alde estuary at Orford in Suffolk, and look back at the imposing castle keep in the town and understand exactly why Henry II decided to build such a splendid fortification here. From the Stone Age to the Second World War, there are walks throughout this book to interest everyone.

Each route, arranged chronologically, has been specially chosen to highlight a particular moment in the counties' dramatic history. All are circular and grid references are given for the starting point. Sketch maps are included for your guidance but, for more detail, it is strongly recommended that you carry the relevant Ordnance Survey map. Convenient car parking places have been noted for all the walks but where roadside parking is indicated, please do so with consideration for other road users and take care not to block any entrances or exits.

There is also a note in each chapter indicating where refreshments can be obtained but it is always advisable to carry a snack with you, and more importantly a drink, particularly on the longer walks. Remember also, that at certain times of the year, paths can be muddy so it is sensible to wear stout shoes.

I do hope you enjoy these walks into history and gain as much pleasure from them as I have had in devising them. Happy walking!

John Wilks

WALK 1
GRIMES GRAVES – INDUSTRY IN THE STONE AGE

Length: 7 miles

Weeting Castle has lain abandoned since the 14th century

HOW TO GET THERE: The walk starts from the Saxon Inn at Weeting. Weeting is on the B1106, 1 mile north of Brandon.

PARKING: There is ample roadside parking around the Saxon Inn, but please park with consideration for residents.

MAP: OS Landranger 144 (GR 773888).

INTRODUCTION

This walk from the village of Weeting, with its ruined castle and old, interesting church, follows tracks and lanes through fields and woods to reach the fascinating Neolithic site of Grimes Graves which is open to the public. It returns through a part of Thetford Forest and across the historic Brecklands to Weeting. Although quite a long walk, the terrain is totally flat and good underfoot.

THE HISTORICAL BACKGROUND

A popular misconception about Stone Age man is that he was a primitive being, clad in skins and living in a cave. In fact, by the Stone Age or Neolithic era, man had developed a sophisticated social organization, with complex religious beliefs. Nowhere is this better illustrated than at Grimes Graves, already an industrial and religious site 5,000 years ago.

Until about 4500 BC, man had been a nomadic hunter-gatherer, living off the land. Significant changes were gradually taking place, however. Man learnt to plant and harvest crops and raise domestic animals. He settled down in semi-permanent dwellings and raised stone monuments to his dead and perhaps also to his gods. He developed specialized industrial sites, at the centre of far-reaching trade routes. Flint became a prized commodity. It was a hard rock that at the same time flaked easily, highly suitable if worked correctly for turning into sophisticated tools. Across England there were a number of sites where flint was mined and then turned into tools and weapons before being traded throughout the country. One of the biggest of these sites, although amongst the last to be developed, was Grimes Graves.

Mining started in earnest at Grimes Graves around 2300 BC and during the next 500 years over 400 mine shafts were dug, covering an area of over 50 acres. Mining and flint-working were specialized

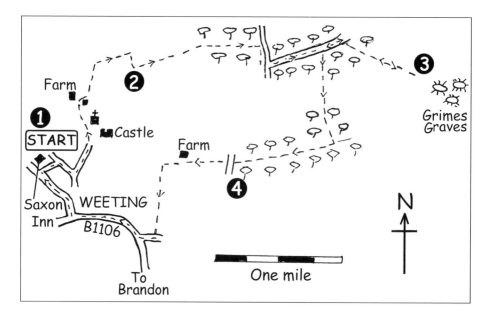

skills, and would have required a large supporting infrastructure to produce food for the workmen. There was thus an extensive farming community adjoining the mining area. Grimes Graves was also the focus of trade routes stretching across England, and therefore supported a market and commercial centre.

The arrival of metal working techniques during the Bronze Age made flint increasingly redundant and, around 1800 BC, the mines were finally abandoned. The refilled shafts left shallow craters that have given the area a strange dimpled appearance, leading later Anglo-Saxons to believe it was the work of the earth-god Grim. In consequence they named the area Grim's Graves. Although modern archaeological excavation has revealed many of the secrets of Grimes Graves, its unearthly landscape continues to fill the visitor with awe and wonder.

THE WALK

❶ With the Saxon Inn on your left, and your back to the main road, walk along the wide side road, Saxon Place. At a T-junction with Herewards Way, turn right and follow All Saints. Where the road bends right, turn left into a side road, signed 'Weeting Castle'. Continue along the road. Where the tarmac ends, keep ahead along a sandy track, soon reaching Weeting Castle and St Mary's church.

Although with the arrival of the Bronze Age, flint ceased to have any use for tool-making, it continued to be of importance in building, especially here in Norfolk. Weeting Castle and church are both magnificently faced with flint.

Weeting Castle was built in the 1130s by Hugh de Plais who held the lands around as a tenant of his overlord, William de Warrenne. Hugh built a sturdy two-storey hall, a miniature replica of de Warrenne's home at Castle Acre (see Walk 4). The whole ground floor of Weeting Castle was an undercroft or storeroom, whilst the upper floor was divided into a great hall and a private chamber. Entry was at first floor level, via a covered exterior staircase. In the 13th century the castle was extended by adding a kitchen range, and a moat was dug around the building. At the same time the outer walls were totally faced with local flint. The castle was abandoned in the 14th century.

Next door to the castle, the church of St Mary, with its distinctive tower typical of many Norfolk churches, is also faced with flints. So prevalent were flints in this area that they were used in many buildings, private homes and farms, as well as castles and churches, a lasting reminder of the

A flint axe head. Grimes Graves was one of the biggest flint mines of Stone Age Britain

industry for which nearby Grimes Graves was famous throughout the country in Neolithic times.

Continue along past the church, and follow the track into a farmyard. Turn right with the track, towards silos. Turn left in front of the silos and continue along the path. At a corrugated iron barn, turn right with the track, passing with the barn and cottage to your right-hand side. At a T-junction of tracks, turn right. Some 100 yards later, at another T-junction, with a house on your right, turn left and follow the leftmost of two tracks.

❷   Follow the track along the left edge of a large field, with woods close on your left, and at the end continue into woodland.

These woods are part of Thetford Forest, a small survivor of the huge forests that covered much of the British Isles in Neolithic times. The main trees in this area were oak, lime and hazel, trees that flourished in the sandy soils of Breckland, as this area of south-west Norfolk and north-west Suffolk is known. The first settlers in the area were few in number, and they cleared small patches of forest to provide arable land. It was not until the Iron Age, around 500 BC, that the population and hence the demand for food had grown sufficiently for widespread clearance of the forest to be required.

Keep ahead through the woods for ½ mile to reach a busy main road. Turn right along the wide grass verge for 250 yards, and then cross the main road with care to turn into a side road, signed 'Grimes Graves' and 'Walt Toft'. Walk along the side road, keeping to the right-hand verge, for ½ mile. Pass a sandy track on your right, signed 'Military Firing Range Keep Out', and continue along the road for a further 200 yards, to reach a stile and fingerpost on the right. Cross the stile and follow a clear path through the woods. Where the path emerges from the trees, keep ahead on a clear track across grassland.

In the late Iron Age the forests were cut back to provide farmland, mainly for the cultivation of cereals, but the thin soils and low rainfall meant that yields were poor. Fields were only used for a few years and then abandoned. In their place, a characteristic heathland developed, with heather on the more acid soils and grassland where it was more alkaline. This pattern of land use continued, with parts of the heath being farmed for short periods and then abandoned again. In the Middle Ages the term 'Breck' was used to describe fields cultivated for a limited time and then left fallow, and this area became known as 'Breckland'.

Follow the track down to a kissing gate. Go through the gate and bear half left on a clear path. Follow the path between a plantation on your right and scattered trees on your left, to reach a stile. Cross the stile and keep ahead on a distinct path across grassland to the entrance hut of the Grimes Graves site seen ahead. This area is designated a Site of Special Scientific Interest, so stay on the path.

Flint was first mined at Grimes Graves around 3000 BC, although only intermittently. It was in regular use as a flint mine from 2300 BC to 1800 BC, with roughly one mineshaft dug each year. A team of up to twelve miners would dig as deep as 30 feet down through the chalk to reach the seam of flint, building wooden platforms and ladders, and using picks made from the antlers of red deer, possibly supplemented with wooden shovels. Once the flint was reached, lateral galleries were dug out from the bottom of the shaft, following the seam and extracting the flint. The galleries were no more than 4 feet high, often as low as 2 feet, and up to 25 feet long. Excavated flints were then hauled back to the surface using ropes and baskets.

Mining started each year in the spring. Up to 1,000 tons of chalk had to be removed from each shaft before the flint was reached, work that could take up to six months. Flint would then be feverishly excavated until either the seam ran out or, more likely, the winter rains led to the shaft flooding and being abandoned. In a good year up to eight tons of flint could be mined. During the winter months when mining was impossible the flint was worked into as many as 10,000 axes. The following spring a new shaft was started, the spoil from this being carefully put back into last year's abandoned shaft. A total of 433 mineshafts were opened and then refilled at Grimes Graves, covering an area of over 50 acres.

There is much speculation that Grimes Graves was of religious as well as industrial importance. The mines burrowed deeper into the ground for the flints than was necessary, at great and on the face of it unnecessary effort. Many axes, made with great precision and artistry, were never used but simply stored. Disused mine shafts were also refilled with far more care

REFRESHMENTS

The Saxon Inn at Weeting is a modern pub, with a beer garden, offering a range of beers; food is available every day. Telephone: 01842 815535.

and tidiness than simple spoil disposal required. It is conjectured that the excavation of flint deep under the soil, and the careful refilling of the shafts, had some religious significance, possibly involving worshipping or paying homage to an earth-mother.

Grimes Graves is open daily from the beginning of March until the end of October, 10 am to 6 pm (5 pm in March and October). There is an entrance charge; free to English Heritage members. One of the deeper mineshafts can be descended and the flint-galleries viewed.

❸   To continue the walk, start by retracing your steps to the road: from the entrance hut go half left along the edge of the car park and across grass to the stile, then follow the clear path to the kissing gate, over grassland and through the trees to the road. Turn left along the road for 200 yards, back to the sandy track and the 'Military Firing Range Keep Out' sign. Turn half left into a clear grassy track, vehicular access barred by a yellow-and-black pole (this is a public footpath, although there is no footpath sign). Do NOT enter the Firing Range. Follow the track. Ignore a cross track but keep ahead, with open ground to left and right. At the end of the open ground ignore a cross track but keep ahead through woods for ¼ mile to reach a T-junction with a broad sandy track. Turn right along the sandy track and follow it for ¼ mile to reach a main road.

❹   Cross the road with care and then keep ahead along the sandy track opposite (ignore a footpath sign pointing to the right). Follow the track past a farm on your right. Just beyond the farm, keep ahead on a sandy track, aiming for woods ahead. At a cross track, with a small wood front-right, turn left and follow a track across a large field, aiming just to the right of a solitary tree mid-field. Keep ahead, aiming to the right of a stand of trees seen ahead. Pass the trees and keep ahead along a clear track, soon passing a small water-filled quarry. Follow the track to go through a kissing gate beside a field gate, and turn right along a lane. In 200 yards, turn right at a T-junction, signed 'B1105 Methwold'. Follow the road, using pavements, for ¾ mile. Ignore a side turn to the left to Hockwood, pass the village green of Weeting, and follow the lane back to the Saxon Inn.

WALK 2
CAISTOR ST EDMUND AND THE ROMAN OCCUPATION
Length: 3½ miles

A bastion tower at Venta Icenorum with the baths beyond

HOW TO GET THERE: The walk starts at the Wildebeest Arms in Stoke Holy Cross. It can be reached either from the A140 to its west or from the B1332 at Poringland.

PARKING: In the side streets of Stoke Holy Cross, but please park considerately. Alternatively, park at the Roman town of Venta Icenorum and start the walk at point 3.

MAP: OS Landranger 134 (GR 235019).

INTRODUCTION

This short circuit starts in the tranquil village of Stoke Holy Cross and goes across farmland and along quiet country lanes, to reach the Roman city of Venta Icenorum. After exploring the city, the walk returns down a country lane to the start. The terrain is flat throughout.

THE HISTORICAL BACKGROUND

Near to modern Caistor St Edmund is the impressive site of Venta Icenorum, a vivid reminder of the splendour of the Roman Empire. Much of the genius of the Romans lay in sharing the material benefits of their civilization with the people they conquered, thereby giving them a stake in preserving the Roman Empire. This policy was not initially followed in the land of the Iceni, modern Norfolk, with disastrous results. The Iceni did not oppose the Roman invasion in AD 43 but instead sued for peace and became a client state. Unfortunately, inept and greedy Roman administrators plundered Iceni land instead of incorporating it into the new province of Britain. This provoked a revolt led by the Icenian Queen Boudicca in AD 61, a conflagration that engulfed much of southern England.

After the revolt was suppressed, new administrators were given the task of winning the hearts and minds of the Iceni. Central to this policy was a lavish new town built at the Icenian capital, to encourage industry and trade and bring prosperity to the region. Planning for this town started in AD 70. It was called Venta Icenorum, meaning 'market place of the Iceni'. A rich, luxurious and successful city soon emerged, ample demonstration of the material benefits of the Roman Empire, and within a few generations of Boudicca's revolt, the Iceni were completely romanised.

By the middle of the 3rd century, Britain faced a new threat, this time from Saxon raiders who crossed the North Sea for plunder. To counter this threat, the Romans built coastal defences, called the Forts of the Saxon Shore. Two such forts were built to command the Yare estuary (now long since disappeared under the silt at Great Yarmouth). These forts, at Caister and at Burgh, protected the sea route to Venta Icenorum. Further protection was given to the city in AD 270 when defensive walls were built around the town. Although it was never attacked, the tranquillity never returned to Venta Icenorum.

In AD 410, the Romans withdrew from Britain and the way was open for an influx of Saxons, initially as raiders but soon as settlers. The existing Romano-British population was either driven out or incorporated into Saxon society. The Saxons were farmers, not town dwellers, and Venta Icenorum was left as a deserted and haunted ruin. Gradually however, the Saxons started to move into the abandoned Roman towns. Venta Icenorum was occupied from as early as AD 450. The Saxons called it 'Castra', a name they gave to

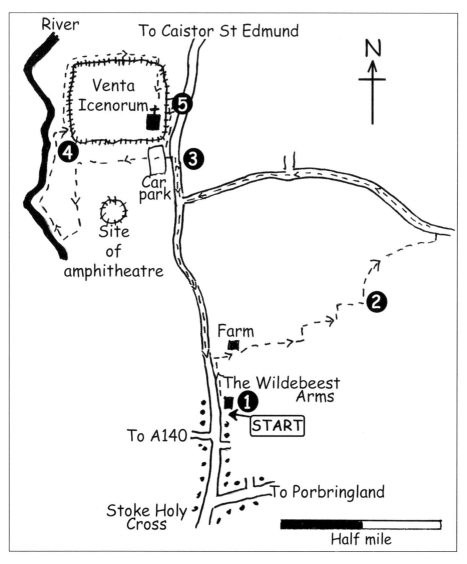

any fortified place, and much later added the suffix 'St Edmund' after the martyred King of East Anglia.

THE WALK

❶ With your back to the Wildebeest Arms, turn right and walk along the road. At the Salmanca guesthouse on your right, turn right onto a concrete drive at a footpath sign. Keep to the right of the gate into the farmyard. Follow the fence for 5 yards, then cross a stile. Keep straight on along a farm track, passing barns on your left. At a metal farm gate turn left through a wooden pedestrian gate. Go forward, with the hedge on your left, through a gateway into the next field. Turn right and walk along the field boundary, with the hedge on your right. Follow the field boundary around two sides to a stile in the corner. Cross the stile and keep ahead, with the hedge still on your right. In the next corner, turn right over a stile. Keep ahead, the hedge now on your left. When the hedge ends, turn left for 40 yards.

❷   At a solitary ivy-covered tree, go half-right across the next large field, aiming for the end of a line of trees seen ahead. On reaching the trees, bear half-right and walk along the left-hand field boundary, aiming for buildings seen ahead. On reaching a hedge, turn left for 20 yards and go through a gap in the hedge onto a lane. Turn left along the lane for ½ mile, ignoring a lane off to the right. At a T-junction, turn right for 600 yards to reach the car park for Venta Icenorum.

❸   Go straight across the car park to a kissing gate (*not* the kissing gate at the far end of the car park leading towards the church). Walk across the field to the link fence ahead. Keep forward, with the link fence close on your left.

To your right are the town walls of Venta Icenorum. For 200 years the town had no walls, and steadily grew until it covered much of the land to your left as well as the right. The walls were built in AD 270 in the face of the threat of Saxon raiders coming inland from the coast. They were only built around the town centre, to protect the main civic buildings and the homes of the wealthy. An extra line of defensive walls was later built to your left, roughly parallel to the link fence. These were nowhere near as high or solid as the main walls to your right, and no trace of them is visible today.

At the end of the fence turn left and continue, the fence still on your left, to a stile by a gate. Cross the stile and keep ahead, with the fence and hedge on your left.

In the field on your left is the site of a Roman amphitheatre (a hollow depression in the middle of the field can just be made out). It was used for athletic events, horse and chariot racing, and also theatrical performances and gladiatorial combat. Every Roman town of any size had an amphitheatre to provide amusement for the population.

The Icenian Queen Boudicca led the revolt against the Roman invasion in AD 61

Pass through a gate into the next field and maintain your direction to a field corner. Here turn right and walk, with the fence close on your left, to reach the river. Turn right and follow the riverbank for a third of a mile, closing in on the walls of Venta Icenorum.

This is the river Tas, which joins the Yare 2 miles north of here and from thence flows to the sea. In Roman times this river was much wider. Ocean-going boats were able to sail into the estuary of the Yare, between the protective forts of Burgh and Caister, and then their cargo was transferred to river boats and brought all the way upstream to Venta Icenorum. The meadows to your right, between the river, the amphitheatre and the walls, would have been covered with buildings in the town's heyday.

On reaching a tower of masonry, clearly visible off to your right, ignore the stile ahead and instead turn right up to the wall.

Just behind the masonry tower was the site of the Roman baths. Every community had a bathhouse, an important building that was used for relaxing and meeting friends, as well as getting clean. The Romans were masters at civil engineering, and the location of these baths is a splendid example of their genius. Fresh water rose from springs in the low hills on the far side of the city, flowed by gravity down the slight slope and through the town, providing water for drinking and washing, before eventually reaching the bathhouse here. Waste water from the city then drained out through the walls, down the slope behind you, before emptying into the river.

❹ Turn left along the old wall.

On the riverside to your left were the old Roman quays. Venta Icenorum was a major trading town, and goods from as far away as Africa and Turkey were brought here and traded for local produce. The meadow between the walls and the river would have been covered with shops and warehouses.

At a corner turn right and continue along the route of the walls, to reach a gate.

This is the site of one of the Roman town gates. Each of the walls of Venta Icenorum was roughly one kilometre long, and each wall was pierced by a strong gate roughly halfway along its length. Two Roman roads, the arteries for trade and communication in the Empire, met at Venta Icenorum. One, from the Midlands, entered through this, the western gate and exited though the eastern gate on the other side, on its way to the coast. The other road ran north to south, from the north coast at Branchester, south to Colchester.

Go through a gate and turn left down the slope, then immediately turn right and walk below the town walls.

This is the most impressive section of the Roman town walls that remains. The walls were 23 feet high, and 14 feet thick, topped with a parapet and walkway. On the outside of the wall was a further defence, a deep ditch. The walls were built of alternating layers of stone and brick for additional strength. It speaks highly of the skill of those Roman engineers that after 1,700 years the walls are still standing.

Walk below the most spectacular length of the Roman wall, and then climb steps back onto the top of the wall.

From this point we can get a clear view over the centre of the Roman town. The walls enclosed a roughly square area of 35 acres, about half of Venta Icenorum. In the very centre of the town, where the two main roads met, was the market square, the forum. Around this were grouped the main civic buildings, the Agora (where the town council met), the Governor's Palace, and the town's two main temples. The rest of the area enclosed by the walls contained other civic buildings and the houses of the town's richest citizens. The bathhouse, in the far right-hand corner, and the forum, were originally built around AD 150. Much of the town was destroyed by fire in

AD 200 and subsequently rebuilt on a far more lavish scale.

Follow the wall around towards the church, eventually dropping down with the path to a kissing gate into the churchyard.

Venta Icenorum was one of the first Roman cities to be reoccupied by the Saxons, and when they converted to Christianity a church was built here, on the site of an old Roman temple. It is not known to which gods the town's temples were dedicated. It seems likely one was Neptune, god of the sea, a popular god with sea-faring traders. Evidence for this is a lead scroll, discovered near the quays, a plea offered by a merchant to Neptune for the return of goods stolen from him, and for vengeance on the thief.

The present Saxon church was dedicated to St Edmund, a Christian king of East Anglia, who was martyred by the Danes for refusing to renounce his religion.

❺ From the churchyard, climb the steps beside the gate you entered by, go over the wall and down steps into the moat.

An additional defence for the Roman town was a massive ditch, 80 feet wide and with an embankment 17 feet high on the outer side, which was dug outside the huge stone town walls. You are now standing in that Roman ditch.

Turn right and follow the moat back to the car park. Exit the car park and turn right onto the lane. Ignoring a lane coming in from the left, follow the lane, soon with a pavement on the right, back to the start.

WALK 3
SUTTON HOO AND THE TREASURE OF THE SAXONS

Length: 6 miles

Astonishing treasures were found when the Saxon grave at Sutton Hoo was excavated in 1938

HOW TO GET THERE: The walk starts from a free car park on the B1083 Woodbridge to Bawdsey road, 1 mile north of Sutton and 3 miles south of Woodbridge.

PARKING: As mentioned opposite.

MAP: OS Landranger 169 (GR 305476).

INTRODUCTION

This varied walk passes the famous Sutton Hoo Saxon burial ground which is open to the public, goes across sandy heathland, and through woods, riverside paths and farmland. Underfoot is mostly easy, although the route can be overgrown in places in summer, and there is one short ascent. Route-finding is quite easy, although care needs to be taken in a couple of places.

The Historical Background

'The Dark Ages', the period between the departure of the Romans in AD 410 and the arrival of the Normans in 1066, were by no means as dark as they have been painted, as the spectacular finds at Sutton Hoo prove.

Throughout the second and third centuries AD the Germanic inhabitants of Denmark, Germany and Holland (loosely known as 'Saxons') sought new lands to live in. This was forced upon them by the twin pressures of increasing population and the encroachment into their homeland from the east by the warlike Huns. When the Romans finally abandoned the province of Britain in AD 410, the way was clear for Saxons in ever increasing numbers to cross the narrow seas.

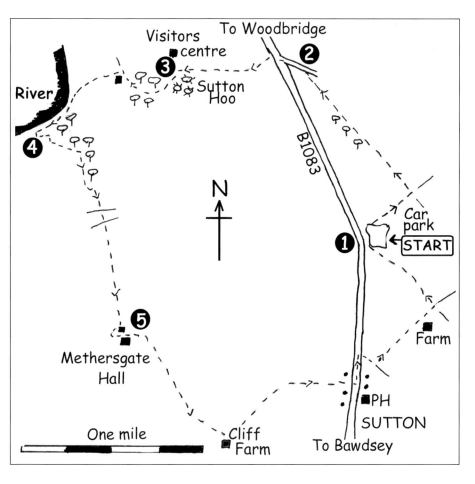

The Saxon settlers initially formed extended family groups, gradually combining under powerful military leaders into a multitude of small kingdoms, which coalesced into larger units. It was at this time that 'East Anglia' – the land of the East Angles – got its name, sub-divided into the lands of the north and south people or 'volk' (Norfolk and Suffolk). The Saxons were essentially a rural people, living in small farming communities. They were pagan, not Christian, had no money economy, trade was by barter, and writing was a rare skill. The cities of the Romans fell into decay. The existing Romano-British inhabitants were either forced westwards or assimilated into the new Saxon kingdoms.

By the end of the 6th century the kingdom of Kent had come to dominate southern England, with East Anglia a client state under its ruler Raedwald. The rest of Britain was largely controlled by the kingdoms of Northumbria and Mercia. In AD 616 Edwin, an exiled Northumbrian prince, fled to East Anglia and sought the protection of Raedwald. King Oswald of Northumbria demanded that Edwin be handed over to him, but instead Raedwald assembled an army, overthrew Oswald and placed Edwin on the Northumbrian throne. With Northumbria now his client, Raedwald soon demanded and received the allegiance of his previous overlord, the king of Kent. Raedwald strengthened his position with judicial marriage alliances, and was soon elected 'Bretwalda', or overlord of the Saxons. On his death in AD 625, Raedwald's stepson Sigebert continued to make East Anglia the pre-eminent Saxon kingdom, overthrowing Mercia and converting to Christianity.

In 1938 a Saxon grave at Sutton Hoo was excavated, revealing treasures of astonishing wealth and sophistication. It has never been established with certainty whose grave it was, but the most likely candidate is King Raedwald.

THE WALK

❶   With your back to the entrance to the car park, walk left around the perimeter track, turning right in 20 yards, then taking the track immediately ahead of you, marked with a finger-post as a byway.

The Saxons were not the uncouth barbarians made out to be by commentators at the time. The Saxons left no written record of their social and political organization, and what we have in the way of written records come from Christians and Romano-British commentators, who naturally had a biased viewpoint. The Saxons were skilled artisans and metal-workers, and developed well-structured systems of law and religious belief. They lived for the most part in small farming communities of just a few families, in simple wooden huts, surrounded by their fields. The heathland you are walking across would have been farmed by such a community, living at nearby Sutton.

Follow the track for 600 yards, then turn left through metal gates. The right of way goes quarter-right across the right-hand field, aiming at the end of a line of trees seen on the far side. (If the field is under crops, you may be better to follow the boundary between the two fields and then, at the end of the fields, turn right for a few yards to regain the route.) The path crosses the huge field to a post in line with the end of the trees. From the post, go to the right of the trees, to pick up a clear path going quarter-right across the next field. You are aiming just to the right of a triangular road sign, just visible on the far side of the field. As you cross the field your destination, a finger-post, becomes apparent.

❷   Meet a lane at the finger-post. Turn left and follow the lane with care to a road junction. Cross the major road to a green finger-post on the other side. Follow the footpath, with trees on the right and fields on the left. Continue, the path soon becoming a track, along the side of three large fields, to reach a cross-track. Continue ahead, the tumuli of Sutton Hoo on your left.

Sutton Hoo (or 'Haugh' – high place, in Saxon) stands on a prominent ridge. From the Bronze Age onwards burials had taken place here under large mounds, or tumuli, which were visible for miles from across the valley of the River Deben, and provided visual proof of the existence and power of the community that raised such mounds. There are 18 burial mounds on this site, where over a period of 50 years were buried successive members of the house of Wuffing, rulers of the Kingdom of East Anglia. The climax of this series of burials was two huge ship burials. Ships, long boats of the design associated with the Vikings, were dragged up from the river far below, inverted, and a body placed beneath, surrounded by goods. The upturned boat was then buried beneath an earthen mound. This form of ship-burial is rare in England, but has been found in Sweden and Denmark, and displays the presence of close cultural links between East Anglia and those countries.

This helmet was amongst the finds from Sutton Hoo

The largest and richest of these ship burials took place under a boat 89 feet long, a vessel so huge and costly it was undoubtedly owned by royalty. The body buried within it lay on a bier, and was surrounded by objects of military authority – a long, beautifully made sword with a jewelled hilt, an iron axe, spears and a huge shield. By the head was a magnificent helmet, richly decorated and with a face-mask representing a winged serpent. Jewelled buckles and fittings of military dress were beside the body, displaying the finest Saxon workmanship, and around the bier were silver dishes, drinking horns, cooking utensils and other household goods.

Such was the wealth buried here, and the nature of the goods, that the grave could only have been that of an extremely important person, and a great military leader. This has given rise to speculation that it is the grave of Raedwald, greatest king of the House of Wuffing. The nature of the burial is in the ancient pagan tradition, later suppressed by the Christian Church, of a mighty warrior being sent off with his possessions to Woden, god of War. It is certainly likely that Raedwald's conversion to Christianity was diplomatic and not heartfelt.

Sutton Hoo was excavated in 1938. The body and the boat had both long since rotted, with only outlines left in the soil, but the goods were untouched, and can now be seen in the British Museum. They are living proof of the skill and sophistication of Saxon society. The Exhibition Centre reconstructs the ship burial and grave goods, and explains the details of its excavation.

The centre is open daily, Easter to September from 11 am to 5 pm; Wednesday to Sunday 11 am to 5 pm in October; 11 am to 4 pm weekends only the rest of the year. There is an entry charge (free to National Trust members).

To see the burial ground, go left. To visit the exhibition centre, go through the gate on the right.

❸ To continue the walk, keep ahead along the fenced track.

The River Deben can be seen far below. From here the effort required to drag an 89-foot longboat up the slope to the skyline can be appreciated.

At a fork in 250 yards, bear right (left will take you to a viewing platform for a good view of the burial ground). Follow the fenced track downhill through trees, ignoring all side turns. Pass White House and follow the track around to the right, and then immediately turn left down a gravel track, passing a high brick wall with inset gates to your right. The track soon becomes a grassy path. Follow the path down towards the river. Cross a plank bridge and climb steps to the riverbank.

Creeks and inlets such as the River Deben were welcome destinations for the Saxons when they first arrived in England. They provided sheltered anchorages close to rich agricultural land, but still within range of the sea that formed a highway for trade back to the continental homeland. The vessel used in the Sutton Hoo burial, although larger than normal, was still a typical example of a Saxon ship. Timber-built, it had overlapping boards held together with wooden pegs, with a large steerage oar at the stern. It was powered by rowers, 40 in the case of the Sutton Hoo ship, but also had a mast and sail for when the winds were favourable.

The main Saxon settlement in this area was on the opposite bank of the river, at Woodbridge. There is no bridge there, and it is probable the name derives from 'Wood-Burgh', 'the burgh (fortified place) in the woods'.

Turn left along the riverbank, then follow the footpath up into woods. The path winds through trees and bracken, along the side of the river, for 600 yards, before climbing steps into a field.

❹ Turn left up the side of the field. At the top of the slope do NOT take the obvious path into the woods, but instead continue around the field edge, the trees close on your left. At the corner of the wood, turn left onto a sandy bridleway. Continue with trees on your left. In the top corner of the field leave the track and turn right along the field edge, with the trees still close on your left. Ignore two tracks going off into the trees, but follow the boundary of the woods to a corner, turning left around it. Some 10 yards after the corner, bear right on a clear path across the field. On the far side, go through a gap in the hedge onto a track. Cross the track and maintain your direction down the side of a field. At the field end cross a tarmac drive and keep straight ahead along the right-hand edge of two fields to reach a drive in front of buildings. Turn right and follow the track between buildings. Turn left through a small white pedestrian gate set into the white fence on your left and pass in front of the large building, Methersgate Hall (this is a public road, although this is not obvious at first).

❺   Follow the road for 200 yards to a junction, and then turn right. Follow the long straight lane, after ½ mile bearing left with the lane, and soon bearing left again to pass Cliff Farm. Continue along the lane for a further ¾ mile to reach the main road at Sutton. (The Plough Inn is 100 yards down the road to your right.)

The name of this village betrays its Saxon origins. Sutton is derived from 'South-Tun', the 'settlement to the south (of the heath)'.

Turn left up the main road for 200 yards and then turn right at a finger-post along a surfaced track. In 120 yards turn left and continue along another surfaced track. In 500 yards, just after a pig farm, stay left with the main track. Some 200 yards later, at a displaced crossing of tracks, turn left onto a sandy track. Follow this track through bracken for ½ mile back to the car park.

WALK 4

CASTLE ACRE AND THE NORMAN CONQUEST 1066

Length: 5½ miles

Castle Acre – a fine example of Norman town planning

HOW TO GET THERE: Castle Acre is just west of the A1065, 4 miles north of Swaffham. The walk starts outside the Ostrich public house, on the village green.

PARKING: There is ample roadside parking around the green, but please park with consideration for residents. There are also signposted car parks at the castle and the priory.

MAP: OS Landranger 132 (GR 816152).

INTRODUCTION

This walk starts in the pretty village of Castle Acre, and visits the ruins of the castle before crossing fields on pleasant tracks and permissive paths. It returns along the valley of the River Nar to the magnificent ruins of Castle Acre priory. Walking is easy, with no appreciable gradients.

THE HISTORICAL BACKGROUND

After the Norman Conquest in 1066, the paramount need for the new Norman monarchy was to impress upon their Saxon subjects the superiority of Norman culture, and so nip any thoughts of revolt in the bud. Castle Acre is a splendid example of this policy.

William the Conqueror arrived with an army of only 6,000 men, many of them mercenaries who had been dismissed by 1070. The conquest was not followed by a mass influx of settlers into England but was essentially the exchange of one aristocracy for a different one. William won a personal kingdom for himself and then held it by rewarding his followers with lands captured from the defeated Saxons. These Norman landowners now had a vested interest in defending their new estates.

The Normans reintroduced into England the art of building stone castles and fortified towns, lost after the Romans departed. William himself saw to it that a castle was built in every county town, and

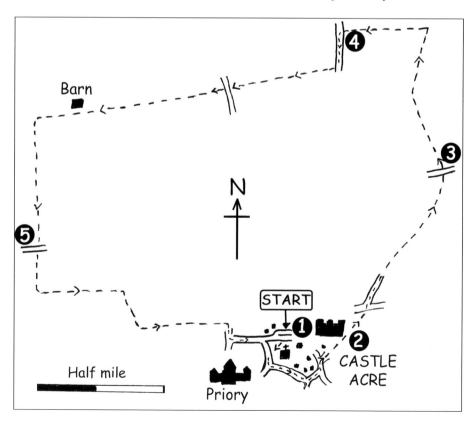

walled towns sat at points of strategic importance. His nobles were allowed a free hand to build private castles to defend their lands. In the years immediately following the conquest a rash of castles sprang up over England.

The Normans were also a genuinely devout people. The Church followed the Norman army into England and, although churchmen were often powerful landowners in their own right, they also set about building churches, monasteries and huge cathedrals as an outward sign of their faith. This Norman ecclesiastical architecture was on a far grander scale than anything achieved by the Saxons.

Castle Acre is the finest example in England of Norman town planning. A new town was built, strategically positioned where the River Nar was crossed by the Peddars Way, a major trade route into the interior of East Anglia. A fortified manor house was an integral part of the defences. Soon a magnificent priory was added. Even today, 900 years later, the splendour of the Norman achievement is still here for all to see.

The Walk

❶ Before starting the walk proper, it is worth detouring a few yards to see the North Gate. With your back to the Ostrich public house, turn left to the end of the village green. The gate is to your right.

Castle Acre was built by the Normans as a fortified town. A high earthen embankment, topped by stone ramparts, surrounded the town, pierced by two gateways. In front of you is the heavily fortified North Gate, which led into the town itself. The town was very small, less than 200 yards on each side, and was confined to the area between this gate and the castle.

To commence the walk, return to the Ostrich. Continue along the village green and turn into the churchyard.

The town wall ran along the left side of today's green, and then turned north, along the boundary of the present churchyard. The church was built outside the walls. The town soon grew, and houses and shops were built outside the walls. The green dates from that later expansion.

Follow the path past the church to a kissing gate in the far corner of the churchyard. Descend steps to a lane and turn left. In 30 yards turn left into Chimney Street. Follow the lane down past houses to a

The Priory at Castle Acre, completed around 1138, was richly decorated

T-junction. Turn left along the lane and 80 yards later, at a second T-junction, turn left again. In 100 yards turn right in Cuckstool Lane.

The bank that can be seen to the left of the main road was part of the original Norman town walls. Over the centuries erosion has lowered it and today it has houses around it, but when first built it would have been an imposing defensive work.

❷ At the end of the lane take the footpath just to the left of the gates to 'The Last House'. Follow the footpath, with the castle ramparts on your left. Turn in here through the ruined curtain wall to visit the castle.

William the Conqueror gave Castle Acre to his loyal supporter, his son-in-law William de Warenne, Earl of Sussex. Around 1080, de Warenne started to build the new town of Castle Acre and here, on the mound of an old Roman fort, he built a fortified manor house. At first glance this building is typically Norman, with a large open space surrounded by strong walls (a bailey), which housed stables, barns and other outbuildings, and within the bailey a fortified accommodation block on a mound (or motte). There are, however, unusual variations to a typical Norman castle. The immensely strong outer walls, which can still be seen today, were an integral part of the town walls, with the southern gate of the town leading into the bailey. On the motte, instead of the traditional fortified keep, de Warenne built a simple two-storey manor house. Since the whole town was Norman, de Warenne's main concern was not protection for his own home from a potentially hostile population, but the protection of the town itself.

(A good example of what this manor house would have looked like can be seen at Weeting Castle, Walk 1.)

During the civil wars of King Stephen's reign (1135–54), William 3rd Earl of Sussex, the grandson of the original earl, thought it necessary to strengthen the fortifications. The manor house was gutted and rebuilt as a strong keep, with thick walls and rooftop battlements. The wall surrounding the keep was raised and thickened, and a dry moat dug around it. The castle was never used as a defensive building and, with the death of the 3rd Earl, the de Warenne line died out and the castle fell into ruin.

The ruins of Castle Acre are open at any reasonable time.

Once you have visited the castle, return to the footpath and continue along the enclosed footpath to a stile leading into a field. Go half left up the field, aiming for a tree at the right end of a row of houses on the skyline. At the tree, maintain your direction, with a fence close on your left. At the end of the fence, maintain the same direction across the field, aiming for the rightmost roof seen on the opposite side of the field.

The mound you are crossing in mid-field is part of an outlying wall, built in Norman times. It stands some distance from the main town walls and seemed to enclose an additional square of land. It is speculated that, as the town expanded, an extra, outer, town wall was built.

Once over the mound a stile comes into sight ahead of you (to the right of the last house). Cross the stile and go through a gate onto a lane. Cross the lane and go up the lane opposite (marked 'Unsuitable for Motor Vehicles'). Where the tarmac ends, keep ahead along a grassy track. In 200 yards turn onto a clear path that leaves the track and goes off right. Follow the path through trees to join a lane.

❸ Cross the lane and go along an unmade track opposite (a DEFRA sign shows that this as a permissive path). Follow the enclosed track past a copse on the left. Continue along the track, now along the edge of a large open field. After 200 yards, and halfway along the field, turn left into a field at a DEFRA finger-post. Walk along the edge of the field, with trees close on your right. At the far end of the field, go through a gate and onto a lane.

❹ Turn left down the lane for 100 yards, and then turn right through a gate onto a broad clay track. Follow this track, hedge on your right, along the edge of two fields. At the end of the second field, cross a lane.

This lane is the course of the Peddars Way. A trackway has followed this route since the Iron Age, connecting the coast near Hunstanton with Thetford, and beyond that Cambridge and eventually London. At the time of the Norman Conquest it was an important trade route, and Castle Acre, a mile south of here, was specifically sited to defend the point where the Peddars Way crossed the valley of the River Nar.

Turn right along the lane for 5 yards, then turn left into a field (marked 'Manor Farm Private Road' but also with a DEFRA finger-post). Go along the tarmac drive, with the hedge now on your left. Where the tarmac ends at a cottage, keep ahead along an unmade track, with the hedge still on your left. Follow the track past a barn and in 300 yards, where the track turns right, go left through a gate (with a DEFRA finger-post). Cross the corner of the field to the hedge line on the left, and follow the hedge. Where the hedge ends keep straight on, aiming for a clearly visible gate at the bottom of the field.

❺   Go through the gate and cross the lane to a gap leading into another field. Enter the field, turn left and follow the boundary, keeping the hedge close on your left. In the corner of the field, where a track comes in from in front, turn right and follow the track down the side of the field, with the hedgerow close on your left. Where the hedgerow ends, keep straight on downhill. At the bottom of the field, turn left and follow the field boundary, with the River Nar just off to your right. At the end of the field go through a gate and turn right along a track. Follow the track for ½ mile out to a lane. Turn right along the lane, with the priory clearly visible ahead of you.

Religion was a living force to the Normans, many of whom were genuinely devout. In 1077 William de Warenne and his wife Gundrada, daughter of William the Conqueror, visited Cluny Abbey in Burgundy and were very impressed by both its beauty and the way in which the Clunaic order was conducted. On returning to England, de Warenne established the first Clunaic priory in England, at Lewes in Sussex, next to his castle there. When Gundrada died in childbirth in 1085, the pious de Warenne established a second priory here at Castle Acre, as a subsidiary of the Lewes Priory.

After de Warenne's death in 1088, his son William, 2nd Earl of Sussex, continued with the vast building work his father had started at Lewes and Castle Acre, and by the time he died in 1138 the priory at Castle

Acre was almost complete. The monks, educated men and able administrators, soon turned to farming as a successful commercial venture, especially sheep farming. The priory continued to gain land from wealthy benefactors, and was exempted from paying taxes by King Henry II, which further added to its wealth. By 1279 Castle Acre Priory supported a prior and 35 monks, as well as many lay brothers, a huge establishment. The buildings of the priory were expanded, lavish apartments were built for the prior, and the whole complex was richly decorated, especially the splendid priory church.

Castle Acre Priory remained the property of its parent Abbey of Cluny, and during the 14th century, when England was at war with France, its fortunes declined. It was fined heavily and many of its rights curtailed, until in 1373 its status was changed from being 'alien' to being part of England. The priory continued to flourish until 1537, when Henry VIII dissolved the monasteries.

Castle Acre Priory is open every day, from 10 am to 6pm from the end of March to the end of October; 10 am to 4 pm November to the end of March. There is an admission charge (free to English Heritage members).

To return to the start, turn left along Priory Road for 200 yards.

WALK 5

BUNGAY CASTLE AND THE STRUGGLE BETWEEN STEPHEN AND MATILDA 1135–53

Length: 5 miles

Bungay Castle enjoyed an excellent defensive position

HOW TO GET THERE: Bungay is just off the A143. The walk starts from the Buttercross, a distinctive open-sided round shelter in the centre of Bungay.	**PARKING:** There are several pay-and-display car parks in Bungay.	**MAP:** OS Landranger 134 and 156 (GR 336898).

INTRODUCTION

This walk starts in the historic town of Bungay and crosses water meadows to the suburb of Earlham. It follows quiet lanes and footpaths, with views over Outney Common, through woods and over meadows to return to Bungay. The castle can be visited at the start or end of the walk. The terrain is mostly flat, with one short uphill section.

HISTORICAL BACKGROUND

The civil war between Stephen and Matilda was a time of anarchy, when the nobility of England waged private wars against each other. Bungay Castle, owned by the Earl of Norfolk, was at the centre of such a private war.

In the 12th century the laws of succession to the throne of England were still evolving, and it was not established who would automatically follow on after a king's death. Henry I tried to avoid potential problems by writing a will, nominating his daughter Matilda as his successor. Although the nobles were required to agree to this, Matilda, haughty, imperious and German educated, was not a popular choice, and many preferred her cousin, the charming, courageous but lackadaisical Stephen. When Henry died in 1135, Stephen moved quickly, and within three weeks had himself declared king. He received major help in this from Hugh Bigod, Earl of Norfolk, who swore that Henry had renounced his will, thereby releasing the nobles from their oath. Matilda promptly raised an army to contest her cousin's coup d'etat, and England was plunged into a state of anarchy that lasted 18 years.

To view the conflict as simply a civil war between the royal cousins is wrong. Many nobles had resented the domination exerted by the Crown under Henry I, and wanted independence from royal authority. They did not care really whether the arrogant Matilda or the mercurial Stephen was on the throne, but saw the anarchic situation as the opportunity to extend their own fiefdoms, pay off old scores and fight local vendettas.

Hugh Bigod epitomized this attitude. Hugh, who had been made Earl of Norfolk by Henry I, preferred to call himself 'Earl of East Anglia', for his ambition was to make that area his own. Hugh initially nominally supported Stephen (it was his perjury that had given Stephen the crown), whilst extending his control over Norfolk by waging war on rival nobles. Bungay Castle, with its access to the sea and to Flanders with its hired mercenaries, became Hugh's major base. His private war increasingly brought him into conflict with Stephen's son, William, a major landowner in East Anglia, and in 1141 Hugh switched his allegiance to Matilda. Stephen seized

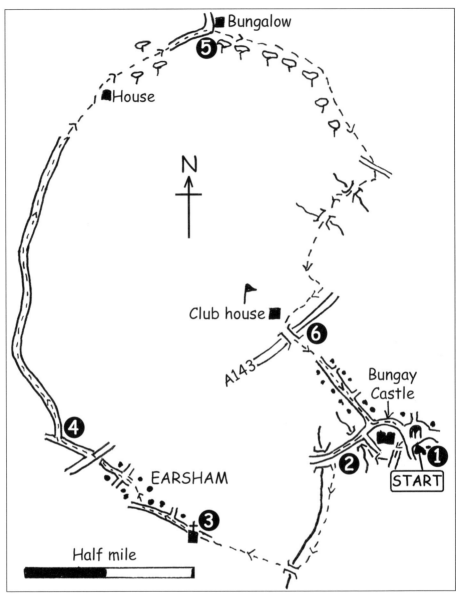

Ipswich from Hugh, Hugh attacked royal castles in Lincolnshire, royal authority diminished, and Hugh Bigod grew in power. Even after the civil war ended in 1153, and Matilda's son became King Henry II, Hugh still clung to the independence he had gained. Four years later he joined a rebellion against the new king. Although the rebellion failed, such was Hugh's power that he escaped punishment.

Hugh Bigod remained the major power in East Anglia for another 17 years. Only then was the king strong enough to move against him (see Walk 6). When Hugh again rebelled in 1173, he was crushed, his castles, including Bungay, confiscated, and he was crippled with a huge fine. Hugh left England in voluntary exile, and died fighting in the Holy Land two years later.

THE WALK

❶ Stand at the Buttercross in the middle of the market square.

There was only a small town at Bungay when the castle was in use, clustered around the market square. The town grew during the Middle Ages as a centre of trade. It was devastated by fire in 1688 and largely rebuilt, and prospered throughout the 18th century. The market cross, or 'buttercross' as it is known, was erected in 1689, as part of the town's regeneration. The symbolic figure of justice was placed on the roof in 1754.

With your back to the Buttercross, cross the road and turn left, passing Martins the Newsagents. Follow the shop fronts around and enter an alley, marked 'Entrance to Bigods Castle'.

At a road, turn right beside the visitor centre/tearoom, and walk along the ivy-covered wall for a few yards to see the castle.

Bungay has always had an excellent defensive position. It stands on a peninsula, surrounded on three sides by the River Waverley, and a castle was first built here by the Saxons. After the Norman Conquest, Bungay was given to William de Noyes in 1070, and later passed to Roger Bigod, Earl of Norfolk. Bigod extensively rebuilt Bungay Castle. The main keep was of stone, with an outer bailey in front of the gatehouse protected by a thick curtain wall. It was this castle that Roger's son Hugh made his base for extending his hold over East Anglia during the reign of Stephen. In 1173 Hugh rebelled against Henry II. A powerful royal army led by Henry himself crushed the rebellion, and Hugh made his final stand in Bungay. The castle was strongly defended by 500 men, but fell when the king's engineers destroyed one of the towers with a mine. Hugh was heavily fined, and Bungay Castle demolished.

The castle we see today was rebuilt in 1294 by another Roger Bigod, this one the 5th Earl of Norfolk. The keep was 70 feet high, its walls 18 feet thick (the thickest castle walls anywhere in England at that time), and a

The conflict between the cousins Matilda and Stephen plunged the country into 18 years of anarchy

strong gatehouse with two semi-circular towers protected the only entrance. An outer bailey (the grassy area that can be seen in front of the gatehouse today) was surrounded by a multi-sided curtain wall and an extra defensive bastion was built in front of the bailey. A drawbridge of revolutionary design was incorporated into the keep; called a 'turning bridge', it was a wooden bridge that pivoted on an axle near its inner end, so balanced that one man could lower it by using his body weight as he walked across it, or raise it by pulling on a single chain. The remains of the former bridge can still be seen today.

Entrance to the castle is via the tearoom/visitors' centre. The castle is open 10 am to 5 pm (noon to 5 pm on Sundays). There is a small entry charge.

After seeing the castle, return to the road and turn right. In 20 yards fork left and 100 yards later, ignore a footpath on the right but 5 yards later, turn right into the recreation field.

The recreation field is in the additional outwork of the castle built in 1294 by Roger Bigod. The curtain wall around the outer bailey was on top of the bank to your right. To your left a further mound marks where an additional wall was built that created an extra bastion for defence.

It is worth walking left across the play area and climbing the steps onto the mound on the far side.

This mound was the support of the wall for a bastion. Beyond the wall the ground drops sharply to the river, a natural moat in front of the castle.

To continue the walk: from the gate into the recreation area climb steps on your right to the top of the bank. Follow the path along the bank and through trees to reach steps descending onto a lane.

This narrow lane follows the course of the ditch that surrounded the castle. The huge curtain wall would have risen above you on your left.

Turn left along the lane for 100 yards to a T-junction (Earlham Street). Turn left, immediately crossing a bridge.

❷   Follow the road, with a pavement on the right, for 300 yards. Just before the next bridge, turn left at a finger-post. Go through a kissing gate and keep ahead along a grassy track, with the stream on your right.

Cross a stile beside a gate and continue through water meadows. Follow the track into a field and keep ahead, following the bank of the stream. At the end of the footpath, turn right and cross a footbridge. Continue along a footpath between hedges to reach a lane. Keep straight on along the lane, over a bridge (the River Waverley) and past cottages. Continue along the lane, now surfaced, to pass the church at Earsham.

❸   Keep ahead for 300 yards, ignoring a road to the right. Just before a red-brick cottage, turn right at a finger-post (the Angles Way). Follow the enclosed footpath out to join a suburban road. Keep ahead for a few yards to a T-junction. Cross the road and maintain your direction along a very short path leading onto a gravel drive. Keep ahead past a social club to reach a road ('The Street'). Cross to the road opposite and keep ahead, passing a pub on your left. Follow the road to a dead end and go through a barrier out to the main road. Cross with care, and keep ahead along the lane opposite (Hall Road).

❹   In 150 yards, turn right into a side lane (Bath Hills Road). Follow this lane for two-thirds of a mile, passing gravel pits on your right. Where the tarmac ends at Valley Farm, keep ahead. Ignore a side turn in 20 yards but keep ahead at a finger-post. Follow the track for 500 yards, with views across the common on your right. Pass through a gate and 20 yards later, at the entrance to a house, bear left and follow an enclosed grassy path around the side of the house. Go through a gate and follow the path through scrubland and into a wood. Follow the path to reach a gate leading onto a gravel track. Go uphill along the gravelled track and at the top of the hill, where the track, now surfaced, turns sharp left, go half right into an enclosed footpath to the right of a bungalow.

❺   Follow the enclosed footpath, eventually turning right and descending. Follow the path along the edge of the escarpment to a stile. Cross the stile and descend to a drive. Cross the drive and maintain your direction to go through a waymarked kissing-gate. At a T-junction of paths turn right. Follow the path across two footbridges and keep ahead to a kissing gate beside a field gate. Cross a culvert and bear half-left to cross a footbridge.

Maintain your direction along a grassy path to a field gate and follow an enclosed grassy track out to a gravel track. Turn left for 40 yards. Do NOT go through the gate onto the road but instead turn right onto a grassy footpath. Follow the path, parallel to the road off to your left, to reach a car park at a golf clubhouse.

❻   Cross the footbridge to the left of the clubhouse and follow the enclosed tarmac path out to the end of a road. Keep ahead along the broad road, passing almshouses and ignoring all side turns, to reach a T-junction. Turn left and follow the road back to the town centre and the Buttercross, passing the Castle Inn.

WALK 6
ORFORD CASTLE –
CONFRONTATION WITH THE
BARONS 1153–1173

Length: 5 miles

Orford Castle was built to a state-of-the-art military design, in 1173

HOW TO GET THERE: Orford is on the B1084 to the west of Woodbridge. The walk starts at Orford harbour.

PARKING: At the pay and display car park at Orford harbour.

MAPS: OS Landranger 156 and 169 (GR 425496).

INTRODUCTION

This enjoyable walk from Orford has an exhilarating section that follows the sea wall along the Alde, with wonderful views over the water meadows, and then returns across fields to Orford Castle which is open to the public all year. The terrain is easy underfoot.

THE HISTORICAL BACKGROUND

The accession of Henry II was by no means trouble-free. He had to work hard to consolidate his position, and Orford Castle is a monument to that work.

In 1153 the power struggle between King Stephen and his cousin Matilda came to an end. Under the terms of the Treaty of Wallingford, that ended the conflict, Stephen would be allowed to reign undisputed for the rest of his life, but on his death Matilda's son Henry would become king. Stephen only lived for another year, and in October 1154, Henry, Count of Anjou and warlord of his mother's forces, became King Henry II, first of the Plantagenet kings of England and founder of a dynasty that ruled for 330 years.

But, upon his accession, the future was by no means certain for Henry. During the 17 years of the civil war, local barons had seized control of much of England and were now used to ruling autonomously. During Stephen's reign 1,115 castles had been built illegally, from which the barons and their private armies dominated the surrounding countryside. Although nominally the barons had sworn allegiance to the new king, many were reluctant to give up the power and independence they had achieved, and all waited to see what Henry would do to establish his rule.

Nowhere was the weakness of Henry's position more apparent than in East Anglia, which was dominated by the powerful Hugh Bigod, Earl of Norfolk (see Walk 5). Although Hugh had sworn allegiance to the new king, his loyalty was at best dubious. When Henry came to the throne, there were only two royal castles in the whole of Norfolk and Suffolk, but he acted with characteristic decisiveness. Seven castles belonging to minor barons were confiscated and rebuilt as powerful royal strongholds, and entirely new castles constructed, the most important of which was Orford. Orford was of major strategic significance. It was close enough to Hugh Bigod's castles at Framlingham and Bungay to counterbalance Hugh's influence, whilst its coastal position meant it could cut Hugh off from the continental mercenaries he was fond of employing.

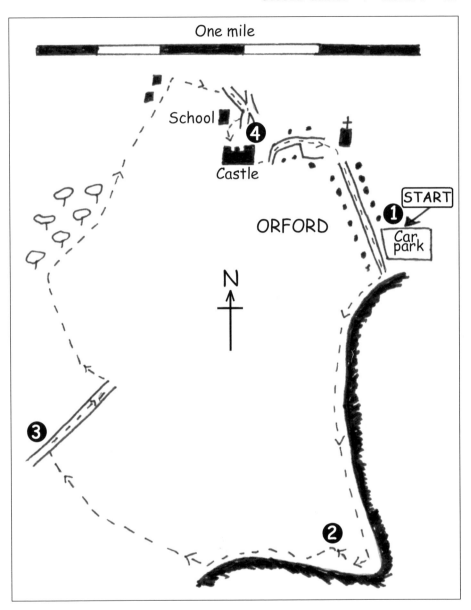

Furthermore, its location meant Orford could be supplied by sea, without danger of being cut off itself.

Orford Castle was completed in 1173, just in time. In that year Hugh Bigod joined a baronial rebellion against Henry who, in turn, acted decisively. The castles of Ipswich, Bungay, Walton and

Framlingham were all taken from Bigod, their defences slighted (deliberately ruined) and the Earl's army disbanded. Although Bigod kept the title of Earl of Norfolk, he was never again a threat to Henry.

THE WALK

❶   From the car park, turn right to the Quay.

In the Middle Ages Orford was a thriving port. The shingle beach of Orford Ness, which can be seen across the water, has been growing larger over the centuries and now runs for over 10 miles south from Aldeburgh, completely blocking Orford off from the sea. In the 12th century, however, the spit was only 4 miles long, extending to just opposite Orford, and providing a sheltered anchorage. The port, which already supported a flourishing coastal trade in all manner of goods, was given an extra boost in 1165, when Henry II started building Orford Castle, for which much of the building material was imported by sea. King Henry modernized the harbour front and built a canal extending into the town centre to allow for easy passage of goods.

By the 14th century the shingle spit had extended southwards sufficiently to make access to Orford difficult. Over the next two centuries the harbour started to silt up, and Orford, no longer of strategic importance, declined into a sleepy fishing harbour again.

Turn right along a path by the side of the estuary. In 100 yards go through a kissing gate and climb steps onto the sea wall.

Orford Ness is one of the longest shingle spits in the country. For many years it was the property of the Ministry of Defence. Martello towers were built upon it as part of the defence against invasion during the Napoleonic Wars (see Walk 14). During the Second World War it was the site of a radar early warning system, and during the Cold War it was used to test triggers for atomic weapons. Today, it is a Site of Special Scientific Interest, and general public access is still denied.

Walk along the sea wall. In 300 yards the path leads over the concrete roof of a Second World War pillbox.

This pillbox is one of many that were built along this coast as part of the defences against coastal invasion.

Continue along the sea wall.   In a further ½ mile, pass through a chain squeeze stile. Ignore a footpath to the right and continue along the sea wall.

All of the land on the right was salt marsh until 1170. By that year Henry II had largely finished building his castle and new town. He now had the first sea wall built and the marshes drained to provide the rich agricultural lane we see today. Henry knew the importance of winning the 'hearts and minds' of the local population, not only overawing them with the splendour of his church and castle, but providing increased prosperity for them to have a stake in protecting. This area is still called the King's Marsh.

❷   Follow the sea wall around the point and continue, soon ignoring an unmarked footpath that comes in from the right.

There are splendid views across the water meadows to the castle and the church, which dominate the landscape for miles around. Henry II was a clever politician and had a firm grasp of human psychology, and these two magnificent buildings provided strong visual symbols of his power in East Anglia.

In a further 600 yards, just after the sea wall turns left, look for a waymark on the bank to the right, with a footpath leading down to a metal gate. Cross the stile and continue along an enclosed green track, out to a lane.

❸   Turn right along the lane for 400 yards and then turn left at a fingerpost, up a sandy lane. Continue for 600 yards to reach woods, and then curve around with the track. Follow it for a further 1,000 yards, until cottages on the left are reached. Just opposite the last wooden shed, turn right onto a footpath into a field (a fingerpost is just visible in the hedge on the right). Follow the footpath between two fields, aiming to the left end of trees seen on the far side, where you enter a track and turn right. Follow the track out to a junction of roads. Bear right past the school onto Mundays Lane and immediately turn right into the recreation field. Go diagonally across the field, aiming for a gap in the hedge in the far corner. Go through the gap onto a track and turn left for 20 yards to reach the castle.

Orford Castle was state-of-the-art military design when it was built. The circular keep, cylindrical on the inside, has a built-on south turret, and in between are three square projecting towers and a forebuilding. This creates 18 exterior sides, defence against the heaviest bombardment possible at the time whilst providing sight-lines for defenders to cover every aspect of the exterior. Inside the keep the accommodation was spacious and luxurious, with chimney-breasts serving to provide central heating to adjoining rooms, and even an en-suite urinal for the castle's constable! Outside the keep was a bailey, surrounded by a strong curtain wall and gatehouse. The whole castle was built from scratch in just seven years, and cost £1,413, equivalent to £2 million today.

Henry's castle had a regular garrison of 30 men, commanded by a full-time constable, although the outer bailey provided the facility to house far more soldiers if the necessity arose. Orford Castle was put to immediate use when a small army, supplied and reinforced by sea, was used to crush the rebellious Hugh Bigod, Earl of Norfolk, in 1173. The castle next saw use in 1217, when it was occupied by the French during the Barons' War, but thereafter the strategic importance of Orford declined. Edward III gave the castle to the Earl of Suffolk in 1336, and it was gradually allowed to decay.

Orford castle is open to the public all year, daily from 10 am to 6 pm, Easter until the end of September; Thursdays to Mondays, 10 am to 4 pm, October to Easter. There is an admission charge (free to members of English Heritage).

❹   After viewing the castle, follow a made-up path to the car park and go out into the street. Go left up the curving street into the market square.

Orford was not mentioned in the Domesday Book, and came into existence as an entirely Norman town. By 1135 it was sufficiently important to receive a licence to hold a weekly market. The town was enlarged and largely rebuilt by Henry II at the same time that the castle was being constructed, a further part of his 'hearts and minds' campaign. A 'new town', with regular streets centred upon a large market square, was laid down. That medieval street pattern survives today.

Continue ahead to reach the entrance to the churchyard. Follow the path to the church door.

REFRESHMENTS

The Jolly Sailor public house is opposite the car park, and has a range of reasonably priced food, including local fish, and has a beer garden. Telephone: 01394 450243. The Crown & Castle in the Market Square, passed en route, has a wider but more expensive range, also including local fish. Telephone: 01394 450205.

There are several other pubs and cafés in Orford.

This is St Bartholomew's church. The first church on this site was Norman, initially a simple structure that gradually grew in size. It was greatly enlarged by Henry II, with the chancel rebuilt and a tower added. Henry's church collapsed in the 14th century and the present magnificent structure, with its 90 ft-high tower, was built on its ruins. The church contains many interesting brasses and is well worth a visit.

From the church door follow the cobbled path down to the street.

This is Quay Street. Once this whole area was marshland, with poor access between the town and the sea along a boggy track. Henry II built a canal which enabled small boats to come right up from the quay to the market square, primarily to bring in building materials for the reconstruction of the castle, but incidentally providing a great boost to trade. Henry also built a raised causeway, where Quay Street now runs, to provide all-weather access between town and quay.

Keep ahead down the street for 400 yards to return to the car park.

WALK 7
PILGRIMAGE TO WALSINGHAM
1070–1538
Length: 5½ miles

Pilgrims would leave their shoes at the Slipper Chapel before completing their journey to Walsingham barefoot

---

HOW TO GET THERE:
Walsingham is 2 miles east of the B1388 Fakenham to Wells road.

PARKING: The pay-and-display car park in the centre of Walsingham.

MAP: OS Landranger 132 (GR 932368).

INTRODUCTION
This walk starts in the historic town of Walsingham, with its abbey and Anglican shrine, and goes across fields and along quiet country lanes to visit the Slipper Shrine. It then returns along a footpath to

Walsingham. The route is on field paths and quiet lanes, with one short ascent.

THE HISTORICAL BACKGROUND

Pilgrimages to a shrine of the Virgin Mary are not generally associated with England, but for 500 years Walsingham flourished as a pilgrimage centre.

In 1061, a rich widow, Richelda de Fervaque, was seeking a way of showing her religious devotion. It is said that the Virgin Mary appeared to Lady Richelda in a dream, took her to Nazareth, and showed her the House of the Annunciation, where the archangel Gabriel had appeared to Mary. She directed Lady Richelda to build a chapel of the exact same dimensions in Walsingham, where the Annunciation could be celebrated by the people of England. Richelda had this vision three times, and eventually built a wooden replica of the House of the Annunciation, the work according to legend being completed by angels when the skill of local carpenters failed.

Whatever its origins, a wooden chapel was built in Walsingham, and the statue of the Virgin it contained soon became an object of pilgrimage. In 1153 Richelda's son Geoffrey founded an Augustinian priory next to the shrine, to cater for the visitors. Walsingham soon became the most popular destination for pilgrims in England after Canterbury, and the only English town to owe its importance solely to pilgrimage. Walsingham's popularity was boosted in 1226, when Henry III came to the shrine, the first of three visits he was to make, and miracles became regularly attributed to 'Our Lady of Walsingham'. In 1381 a later king, Richard II, went further and presented England to 'Our Lady of Walsingham' as her dowry. Royal patronage and pilgrims' offerings made both priory and town rich for the next three centuries.

In 1538 Walsingham Priory was dissolved, as part of the general dissolution of the monasteries. The shrine fell into ruin and, over the succeeding centuries, was largely forgotten. But in the 1890s, Charlotte Boyd, a wealthy Anglican, converted to Catholicism and set about restoring the 'Slipper Chapel', a mile or so outside town and the last wayside shrine for pilgrims journeying to Walsingham, which in 1897 became the destination for pilgrimage again. However, English Catholics showed little enthusiasm for the shrine, and pilgrimage was limited. In 1921, the Anglican vicar of

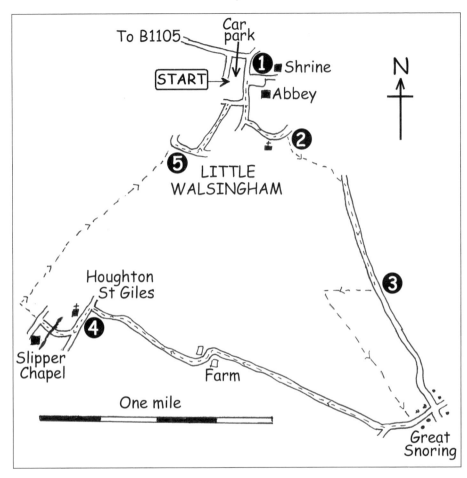

Walsingham, Alfred Hope-Patten, determined to recreate the medieval shrine in the town itself. The popularity of the Anglican shrine reawakened Catholic fervour for renewing the Slipper Shrine, and today Walsingham has become a centre for pilgrimage again.

THE WALK
❶   Leave the car park by the bottom exit and bear right into Common Place.

Common Place is the smaller of two medieval market places. The town pump, its original water supply, is housed in an octagonal conduit house in the centre of the square. The square itself is lined with many half-timbered buildings, dating from the time of the priory although somewhat altered in the intervening centuries. On the south side of the square is the Shire Hall, once the town's guildhall and later its gaol and courtroom. Today, it houses the museum and Tourist Information Centre.

The remains of the Augustinian priory are entered through the museum. Building of the priory began in 1153, when Richelda de Fervaque's work was carried on by her son Geoffrey. He established a religious house to care for the Shrine to Our Lady, and cater for the ever-increasing numbers of pilgrims flocking to Walsingham. The shrine itself stood in the extensive grounds attached to the priory. In the 13th and 14th centuries the priory church was rebuilt on a far more lavish scale, and in the 15th century the wooden chapel housing the holy shrine was replaced by a stone building.

Every king from Henry III to Henry VIII visited Walsingham at least once, and each made generous bequests to the priory, which grew ever wealthier. Somewhat ironically, the last royal bequest was made by Henry VIII. But, as the Reformation gathered pace, enthusiasm for the cult of the Virgin Mary waned. Seeing the writing on the wall, Walsingham Priory was one of the first religious houses to recognize King Henry as Head of the Church in England, signing the Act of Supremacy in 1534. This proved to no avail, however, and in 1538 Walsingham Priory was formally dissolved. The statue of the Virgin was taken to London for burning, the shrine and priory church were demolished, and the land sold to private landlords.

Today little remains of the former priory. A part of the vaulted undercroft and the refectory can be seen built into a Georgian country house, and in the surrounding landscaped park are the dramatic remains of the east end of the priory church.

Entrance to the priory is via the museum, open 10 am to 4 pm at weekends, and 10 am to 4.30 pm weekdays. There are slightly shorter opening times in winter, and the priory is closed in January. There is an entrance charge.

Turn right along High Street, passing the abbey gate on your left.

The massive gatehouse and retaining walls were part of the original priory, and pilgrims would have entered the priory and shrine through these gates.

Walk down the historic main street of Walsingham.

High Street follows the course of the old medieval main street, and is lined with buildings retaining their half-timbered upper storeys, but with flint-faced ground floors dating from the 17th and 18th centuries. At the height of its popularity there were over 20 hostels for pilgrims in Walsingham, and although the town's prosperity declined after the Reformation, the resurgence of pilgrimage in the 20th century has given a renewed boost to the town. Note as you walk down the High Street the sign for the Eastern Orthodox Church, which was established in the town in 1967 in the buildings of the old railway station.

At the bottom of High Street, at a junction of roads, turn left into Church Street. Follow the road over a bridge and past the church.

St Mary's has been the parish church of Walsingham since the Reformation. Although devastated by fire in 1961, the outer walls, porch and tower survived, as did the magnificent stepped font, one of the finest in Norfolk. In 1921 the Reverend Alfred Hope-Patten, vicar of Walsingham and an ardent Anglo-Catholic, placed a statue of the Virgin Mary in a side chapel in this church and set about reviving the cult of organized pilgrimages.

❷   At the far end of the churchyard turn right along a concrete farm track to a farm. Just before the farm cross a stile on the left beside a gate and go half right up the field, aiming at a single oak tree seen at the top of the field, to the left of a wood. As you approach, a stile and gate become obvious behind the oak. Cross the stile and maintain the same direction to a telegraph pole. Keep ahead to a stile in the corner of the field. Cross the stile and turn left for 5 yards to reach a lane. Turn right along the lane, climbing quite steeply for ¼ mile. At the brow of the hill continue along the lane for another ¼ mile, to where a line of trees joins the road on your right.

❸   Immediately beyond the line of trees, turn right onto a green track. A fingerpost, lying in the grass at the time of writing, marks the path (NB: this is a permissive path, open until at least 2008. If permission is revoked after that time, simply continue along the lane for another half a mile to reach the crossroads in the middle of Great Snoring. Here turn right and 200 yards later rejoin the route).

Walk along the green track, trees on your right and a field on your left. At the far side of the field, turn left onto a second green track.

Follow it for 1,000 yards to join a lane, and turn right, signed 'East Barsham' (the lane route, avoiding the permissive path, rejoins here). In 250 yards, ignore a side road to the left but keep ahead, signed 'Houghton 1½ miles'. Follow this very quiet lane, with good views on both sides. In ¾ mile zig-zag between farm buildings, and half a mile later come out to a crossroads.

❹ Turn left, signed 'Fakenham', and follow the road past the church and then turn right down a narrow side lane. Follow the lane, crossing a footbridge beside a ford, out to a T-junction. Turn left to see the Slipper Chapel.

The Slipper Chapel stands on the site of the last wayside shrine on the pilgrimage route to Walsingham, so named because many pilgrims removed their shoes here in order to complete the last 1½ miles of their pilgrimage barefoot. A chapel was opened in 1325 and remained in daily use for two centuries. After the Reformation the chapel was used as a barn. In 1891 Charlotte Boyd conceived her plan to restore Walsingham to its former glory. She converted to Catholicism, bought the chapel and gave it to Downside Abbey. Using funds provided by Mrs Boyd, the Abbey restored the building, and in 1897 a procession of pilgrims journeyed from Kings Lynn to the Slipper Chapel.

English Catholics initially had little taste for pilgrimage. In the three centuries since the Reformation they had become accustomed to pursuing their faith discreetly and privately, and considered pilgrimage and worship at shrines as 'un-English'. It was not until the 1920s, when the Anglican church rebuilt the Shrine to Our Lady in Walsingham itself, that Catholics actively encouraged worship at the Slipper Shrine. The building of the adjoining Chapel of Reconciliation, consecrated in 1982, greatly boosted pilgrimage, and both chapels now have pilgrim hostels attached.

To continue the walk, return to the T-junction. With your back to the lane and ford you came from, keep ahead up a concrete track. In 70 yards, turn right onto a footpath that follows the course of a disused railway. Follow the footpath for 1,000 yards to emerge at the corner of a lane.

❺ Turn right down the lane for 120 yards and then turn left into a narrow side lane. Follow the lane for 400 yards, passing the ruins of the friary on your right.

The Fransiscans established a friary in Walsingham in the 14th century, to capitalize upon the town's growing reputation. The friary was dissolved in 1538.

REFRESHMENTS

The Bull Inn, in Common Place at the start of the walk, is an old pub with additional open-air seating, offering a range of food and beers. Telephone: 01328 820333.

There are several other pubs and tearooms in Walsingham.

At a crossroads, turn right and follow the lane downhill, past the Black Lion, to the High Street. Turn left and follow the High Street back to Common Place and the car park just beyond.

To visit the Anglican shrine, go diagonally across Common Place, following a road to the left of the Bull Inn. The shrine is a few yards down on your left.

The Anglican shrine was opened in 1931, the result of ten years' effort by the Anglican vicar of Walsingham, Alfred Hope-Patten. It is built on the site of the original medieval shrine. The Holy Well, whose waters supposedly have miraculous healing qualities, is located within the shrine, and is today a site of pilgrimage. The present shrine houses an elaborate altar, a curious mixture of Catholic and Eastern Orthodox designed by the church architect, Sir Ninian Comper. The whole complex, with its numerous side altars, statues, and mosaic murals, seems a far cry from the Reformation that swept the original shrine away over four centuries ago.

WALK 8

CASTLE RISING
THE SHE-WOLF OF FRANCE
1331

Length: 4 miles

Edward III 'modernised' Castle Rising in 1331 for his mother Isabella – she lived there until she died in 1358

HOW TO GET THERE: Castle Rising is just west of the A149, 2 miles north of Kings Lynn. The church and almshouses from where the walk starts are reached by following the small one-way system in the village centre.

PARKING: There is ample roadside parking near the almshouses.

MAP: OS Landranger 132 (GR 666248).

INTRODUCTION

This walk starts in the attractive village of Castle Rising, then follows country paths through the surrounding woods before returning to the castle itself. Walking is easy, mainly on tracks, footpaths and quiet lanes, with one short stretch along the main road.

THE HISTORICAL BACKGROUND

Castle Rising became the final home to one of England's more controversial queens, Isabella, the 'She-Wolf of France'.

One of the first acts of Edward II after his accession in 1307 was to marry Isabella, the 13-year-old daughter of King Philip of France, a purely diplomatic marriage aimed to cement relations between the two countries. The new queen, young, beautiful and fashionable, was instantly popular with the English people.

Although intelligent and cultured, Edward II lacked the political and military skills needed by a medieval monarch. He made no secret of his contempt for his powerful barons, upon whose support the

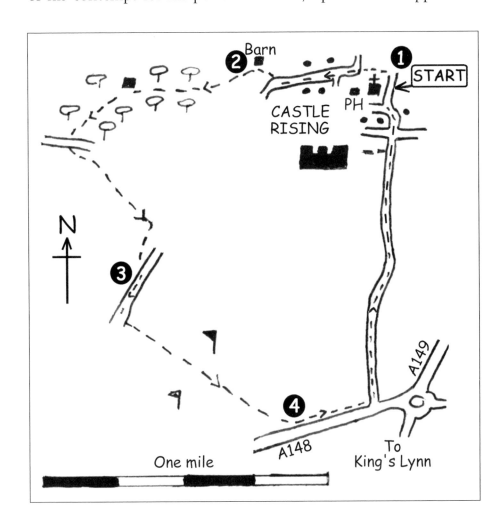

crown depended, and wilfully alienated many of them. Worse, Edward, a homosexual, flaunted his lover Piers Gaveston, lavishing him with honours and encouraging his vicious wit at the expense of the nobility. In 1311 a group of barons known as the Ordainers, led by Edward's cousin, Thomas Earl of Lancaster, rebelled. Gaveston was executed and the king was effectively forced to place the government into the Ordainers' hands. The lot of the teenage Queen Isabella, who had deeply resented Gaveston, seemed improved. Thomas of Lancaster was a friend and ally, and she now had a new son, Edward, born in 1312. King Edward did not, however, learn the lessons of this revolt. A new favourite, Hugh de Spencer, soon emerged, and was given riches and influence. As Isabella matured, so her resentment grew.

For ten years Edward carefully built support amongst those nobles who objected to the Ordainers. In 1321 a revolt erupted in the Welsh Marches led by Roger de Mortimer. This gave Edward his chance. He crushed the rebels, imprisoned Mortimer (who later escaped to France) and had Thomas of Lancaster, his lifelong enemy, executed for treasonably encouraging Mortimer's actions. Edward and his beloved Hugh de Spencer reigned supreme, and Isabella, politically isolated after Lancaster's death, found her position increasingly humiliating and intolerable.

In 1326 King Edward naively allowed Isabella to travel to her native France to visit the new king, her brother Charles, and to take Prince Edward with her. Here she raised an army and returned to England accompanied by Mortimer, who had fled to Paris and was now her lover. Landing near Orford (Walk 6) she marched on London, demanding that Edward step down in favour of his son. To King Edward's few supporters Isabella was the 'she-wolf of France' come to ravish the kingdom, but to many others she was a saviour. Edward was deposed and soon brutally murdered, on Mortimer's orders and with Isabella's tacit approval. The 14-year-old prince was crowned Edward III, but real power lay with Isabella and her lover.

For three years the young Edward III quiescently allowed Isabella and Mortimer to rule England, until he felt strong enough to overthrow them. Then, in 1330 Mortimer was hanged, drawn and quartered for the murder of Edward II. Queen Isabella was imprisoned in Castle Rising for the rest of her life.

THE WALK

❶   Walk along the lane, with the church on your left and Trinity Hospital almshouses on your right.

Trinity Hospital was built in about 1614 by Henry Howard, Earl of Northampton. The Howards had been one of the most powerful families in Tudor England, holding the Dukedom of Norfolk, and owned Castle Rising and much of the land in the vicinity. With the dissolution of the monasteries, there was a need for places of refuge for the aged, and wealthy landowners often built almshouses, or 'hospitals'. Henry Howard built three sets of Trinity almshouses, these in Castle Rising, and companion houses in Greenwich and Clun. The Castle Rising almshouses provided homes for twelve women, aged 56 or more, of good character and able to read. They were required to pray three times a day, and a chapel was built as part of the almshouse complex. Trinity Hospital still accommodates nine female residents, and a tour, guided by the warden or one of the tenants, is very rewarding.

It is open to visitors on Wednesdays and Sundays from 10 am to 12 noon and 2 pm to 6 pm (4 pm in winter). A donation is invited.

Where the wall on the left ends, turn left through a kissing gate, beside a wooden gate. Keep ahead down a drive, a wall close on your left. Go through another kissing gate and keep ahead along the gravel drive. Ignore a road to the right but keep straight ahead along the lane. In ¼ mile, where the lane turns sharp left, go half-right onto an unsurfaced track. Follow the track through a gate and at a barn 20 yards later, fork left.

❷   Follow the track, soon entering light woodland. Just past a house on the right, at a T-junction of tracks, keep straight ahead along a footpath, marked with a finger-post. Follow the footpath out to a lane. Go diagonally right across the lane and then turn left onto a footpath (a finger-post just behind the 30 mph sign marks the way). Immediately fork right, on a path initially parallel to the lane but soon veering away to the right into woods. After 200 yards ignore a side path to the left, but 10 yards later, at a T-junction of paths, bear left. Where a path joins from the left, keep ahead. Some 200 yards later, at a cross-track, keep straight on. Continue on this path through the woods, ignoring paths to right and left. Cross a footbridge and 20 yards later, at a link fence, turn right. Keep ahead along an open sandy area, with a bank on your left, to reach a lane, opposite the entrance to a golf club car park.

❸ Turn right along the lane for 200 yards, then turn left onto a distinct path leading into woods (if you reach a drive saying 'Private The Black Cabin', you have gone 20 yards too far along the lane). Walk with a fence on your right and the golf course off to your left. Where the woodland path joins a gravel track, keep straight on, following the track between fairways. Follow the track for ½ mile, bearing right and continuing along a tree-lined path to reach a main road.

❹ Turn left and walk with care along the busy A148 for 400 yards, keeping to the wide grass verge. Just before the roundabout, turn left onto Lodge Lane. Follow this quiet country lane for ¾ mile to reach the entrance to the castle on your left.

In Saxon days the estates of Castle Rising were part of the property of the archbishops of Canterbury, and a small church and manor house stood on

this site. After the Norman Conquest the estates were given to the Norman archbishop, Odo, but when in 1088 the latter rebelled against King William Rufus, the manor was given by the king to his loyal supporter William d'Albini. The latter's son, known as 'William of the Strong Hand', married into the royal family and became Earl of Sussex. He set about making the manor into a massive castle. Huge embankments were

Queen Isabella landed near Orford before marching against King Edward

REFRESHMENTS

The Black Horse in Castle Rising is a large and spacious pub, with a beer garden. It offers a good selection of local beers and a wide range of food. Telephone: 01553 631225.
  There is also a shop and tearoom in the village.

raised (burying the original church), a deep moat dug, and the massive stone keep was built. At the time of its construction, the keep was the largest in England, and noted for its highly decorated forebuilding and staircase.

Castle Rising was owned by the D'Albinis and their descendants, the de Montalt family until 1329, when the castle, now remote from the political life of England and falling into disrepair, passed to the Crown. It was thus vacant at the time when Edward III was looking for safe accommodation for his mother, Queen Isabella.

After he seized back his crown in 1331, Edward realized it would be inadvisable to allow Isabella to remain at court, or any place where she could play an active part in political life. She was deprived of her estates and instead given a pension of £3,000 a year, a huge sum at that time. Castle Rising was extensively rebuilt and modernized, and Isabella was given a retinue of 180 servants. Although the queen was required to live in Castle Rising under a form of luxurious house arrest, she was given considerable freedom to travel for visits, and the Shrine at Walsingham (Walk 7) became a particular favourite with her.

Edward III's feelings for his mother were ambiguous. He had resented her relationship with Mortimer and the power she had allowed him, and blamed her for involvement in the death of his father. However, he was also well aware of his father's many failings, both as a king and as a husband. His relationship with his mother remained cordial and he visited her several times a year. Nevertheless, Isabella lived in gilded exile at Castle Rising for the remainder of her life. She was 36 when she came to the Castle in 1331, still beautiful and used to being at the centre of cultural and political life. She died, largely forgotten, at Castle Rising in 1358, aged 63.

The castle is open from 10 am to 6 pm, April to end October; 10 am to 4 pm November to March. There is an admission charge (free to English Heritage members).

To finish the walk, continue along the lane to reach a road junction. Keep ahead along the lane opposite, marked 'No Entry'. Follow the lane around to the left, to return to Trinity Hospital, with the church and Black Horse public house in front of you.

WALK 9
UPTON – HOW THE BROADS WERE MADE

Length: 7 miles

St Benet's windmill by the River Bure was used primarily as a pump to drain the surrounding peat excavations

HOW TO GET THERE: Upton is 1 mile north of Acle, signed from that town. Boat Dyke, where the walk begins, is signposted from the middle of Upton.

PARKING: Boat Dyke car park (free).

MAP: OS Landranger 134 (GR 403128).

INTRODUCTION

This walk offers a wide variety of splendid broadland scenery. It starts at Upton, and goes along the banks of Upton Dyke and the River Bure, beautiful waterways alive with pleasure boats. After seeing the ruins of St Benet's Abbey, it returns past South Walsham Broad and then crosses fields and reclaimed land to return to Upton. The terrain is flat and good underfoot.

THE HISTORICAL BACKGROUND

Today the Norfolk Broads are known as an area of outstanding 'natural' beauty. Beautiful they undoubtedly are, but in the last 40 years it has been discovered that they are anything but natural. They are in fact the result of the greatest human modification of the landscape in Britain.

When the glaciers retreated at the end of the last Ice Age, some 12,000 years ago, the area of modern East Anglia was left as a wide, very shallow dome. Its highest point was How Hill, a sand and gravel knoll, a mere 40 feet above sea level, from which the land sloped very gently downhill in all directions. Soggy tundra covered the slopes, which gradually drained to form a thick peaty cover over the underlying sand.

Almost from the time that humans discovered fire, they had found that peat was a rich source of fuel. As the population increased, more peat was dug and burnt. By the 12th century, East Anglia was a rich and highly populated area. Norwich was the second largest city in England. Fuel was in ever-increasing demand, and the monks of St

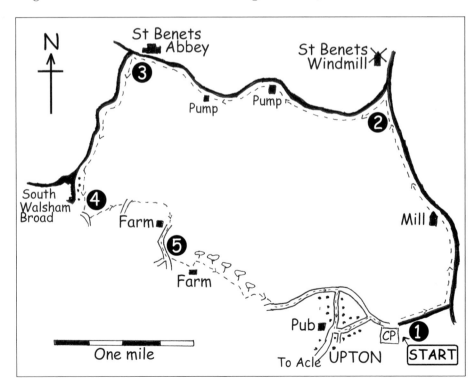

Benet's Abbey, on the banks of the River Bure, were given the licence to commercially extract peat. Turves of peat, roughly one ft square and four inches deep, were dug out by hand and sent along the rivers to Norwich and beyond. The scale of the excavation was huge. In a single year a million turves were cut, with 400,000 turves being supplied to Norwich Cathedral alone. Over the two centuries, 2,600 acres (the equivalent of four square miles) were cleared of peat, in trenches and in large flat quarries, to a depth of up to 12 feet.

Around the end of the 13th century, climate change caused the sea level to rise, not by a great amount but enough to dramatically affect low-lying Norfolk. The flat lands around the meandering rivers were subject to increasing flooding, threatening the peat quarries, many of which were below sea-level. Massive efforts were put into flood defences, with embankments along the rivers and extensive pumping and channelling to drain the land, but in vain. By the 15th century, peat cutting was impossible in the increasingly wet marshlands, and the diggings were abandoned. Gradually the channels and flat basins filled with water, to create the classic Broadland scenery we know today. Over time, the very existence of the peat workings was forgotten, until it became assumed that the landscape was entirely natural. It was not until the late 1950s that research by geo-morphologists discovered that the Norfolk Broads had been created, not by nature, but by medieval monks.

THE WALK

❶   From the car park go to the boat moorings. Walk along the embankment, with the water on your right.

This channel, Upton Dyke, is man-made. The land to your left, Upton Marsh, was once a huge flat lake, but gradual infilling with sediment and dead vegetation over the past four centuries has created a marshland instead. In 1840 there were 3,000 acres of open water in the Broads; today there is only half that amount, the result of infilling, which has been going on since the land was flooded in the 15th century.

To your left, just as you start along the embankment, you will see a very small, windsail-driven, pump. This is a design called a tasker, imported from Holland. Lightweight and mobile, it can be moved around the marsh to remove surplus water from the many drainage ditches. Pumps very similar to this were first introduced by the monks of St Benet's in the 14th century.

Continue along the channel for ½ mile to reach the River Bure. Bear left with the embankment and continue. After ¾ mile pass a disused windmill.

This windmill dates from around 1800, but windmills had been used in this area for the previous four centuries to drain the marshes. The River Bure was first embanked in the 13th century in order to protect the fields and peat workings along its banks.

Continue along the riverbank for a further ¾ mile, to the confluence of the rivers Bure and Thurne.

In front of you is St Benet's windmill. In the 12th century, all this land was part of the manor of Hoveton, the feudal property of St Benet's Abbey. The first windmill was built on this site by the monks of St Benet's and was used primarily as a wind-driven pump, to drain the surrounding peat excavations.

❷   Continue along the embankment for a further ¾ mile, until you reach the small brick building of Doles pumping station.

This pumping station, used to drain water from the surrounding marshland, is a modern design, driven by electricity. The land behind it is actually below sea-level.

Continue along the riverbank for another ¾ mile, passing another small pumping station, to reach the ruins of St Benet's Abbey on the opposite bank.

St Benet's Abbey, a cell of the Benedictine Order, was founded in the 9th century. It was initially only a small establishment, and fell into disuse. It was rebuilt in 1020 by King Canute, and endowed with three manors. After the Norman Conquest the rights of the Manor of Hoveton were given to the abbey in perpetuity. The abbey's wealth blossomed from the 12th century onwards, when it was granted the licence for extracting peat. Peats were loaded onto wherries, large sail-propelled barges, and sent along the River Bure to market in Norwich and beyond. The abbey was abandoned after the dissolution of the monasteries and its land sold to local farmers. The red-brick tower-mill we see today was built into the ruins of the Abbey gatehouse in the 1800s.
The low rise seen on the skyline beyond the abbey ruins is How Hill, at

40 feet above sea level the highest point in the Norfolk Broads. Its name comes from the Scandinavian word 'haugh, meaning 'high', and was given to the hill by Viking raiders who sailed into these estuaries in the 9th century.

❸ Just beyond St Benet's, turn left and follow the bank of Fleet Dyke.

This is another artificial channel, created by the extraction of peat. The land to your left is below sea-level, and only the embankments along the river keep it from being inundated. Even then, constant pumping is required to remove the water that continually seeps to the surface.

After ½ mile, follow the path as it veers away from the dyke for a while before rejoining the bank.

Turn inland with the path and follow it out to a track. Keep ahead along the track, passing boat yards. At the end of the housing and fences on your right, look for a sign saying 'South Walsham Broad'. Go right for a few yards to see the broad itself.

St Benet's Abbey was rebuilt by King Canute in 1020

This large open expanse of water, like all the broads, is, despite appearances, not a natural lake. It is, in fact a vertically sided basin, cut directly down through the natural peat of valley floor, to a depth of up to twelve feet. Often narrow parallel peninsulas and free-standing platforms of peat were left uncut between and within the basins. From the 13th century onwards, the water levels of the sea and the water-table rose, and the basins gradually flooded to create shallow lakes. The lakes, in turn, have gradually infilled with dead vegetation and sediment, not only dramatically reducing their size but also softening their contours until today the broads look just like natural lakes.

❹ Continue past Kingfisher Lane and a car park on your right, bend left with the lane and 20 yards later turn left at a finger-post. Walk along the side of a field, with the hedge on your left. Pass through the hedge and maintain your direction, with the hedge now on your right. Follow the path out to a lane and turn left. In 50 yards pass a cottage on your left and 20 yards later fork right onto a green track. Follow the track to reach a farm. Keep ahead on a surfaced track, passing the farm on your right. In 200 yards, at the entrance to Low Farm, keep ahead along a lane and continue until a road junction comes into sight. Just before the junction, at a green triangle with a sign saying 'Low Road', turn left along a track, passing Hilly Lodge on your left.

❺   Follow the track between Ivy Farm and Holly Farm. Where the track enters a farmyard, turn left at a finger-post onto a green lane. After 50 yards bear left onto an enclosed footpath. Follow the path as it winds along the edge of woods, with Upton Broad off to your left. Continue to follow the path over a footbridge and along the edge of fields. Ignore a turn to the right but continue with the enclosed path through the edge of woods, and then between fields to finally emerge at houses. Keep ahead to reach a lane at Orchard Cottage and turn left. Follow the lane for ½ mile to a junction with Marsh Lane.

For a short-cut back to your car, keep ahead along Back Lane. In 400 yards, at a T-junction, turn left again back to the car park.

To continue into Upton, turn right along Marsh Road for 400 yards to reach the White Horse Inn. Turn left in front of the inn, onto a road signed 'Boat Dyke'. In 100 yards turn right onto Boat Dyke Road. Follow the lane for 350 yards, until a lane joins from the left (the short cut joins here). Continue around to the right, back to the car park.

WALK 10

LAVENHAM AND THE
WOOL TRADE 1420–1520

Length: 4½ miles

The Guildhill in Lavenham has enjoyed a chequered history since it was built in 1528

HOW TO GET THERE: Lavenham is on the A1141, midway between Bury St Edmunds and Hadleigh.	**PARKING:** Use the free car park at the southern end of Lavenham from where the walk starts.	**MAP:** OS Landranger 155 (GR 914489).

INTRODUCTION

This walk starts in the beautiful old town of Lavenham and explores the surrounding countryside, with views dominated by Lavenham's church. It uses field paths and quiet lanes, before returning to explore the town. The terrain is flat and easy underfoot.

THE HISTORICAL BACKGROUND

In the Middle Ages, much of East Anglia's prosperity came from the weaving trade, and nowhere can that medieval prosperity be better seen today than in Lavenham.

In the 14th century, weaving in Suffolk was confined to the area around the Essex border, centred upon Sudbury. The trade received a boost in 1337 when Edward III encouraged Flemish weavers, displaced by the wars in France, to settle in the area, adding their skills to an already flourishing industry. The trade was dominated by the master clothiers or merchants, who bought the raw wool. They then employed spinners and weavers who worked in their own homes to turn the wool into cloth, which the clothiers then sold on. Suffolk's chief product was thick woollen broadcloth, which was widely exported throughout Europe.

Lavenham's hilltop market had always been a major centre for trade, especially wool, but gradually developed an expertise in weaving, especially a product known as Lavenham Blue, a broadcloth dyed with woad. The town's heyday was from 1420 to 1520, when it was dominated by three generations of master clothiers, the Spring family, all confusingly named Thomas. Thomas

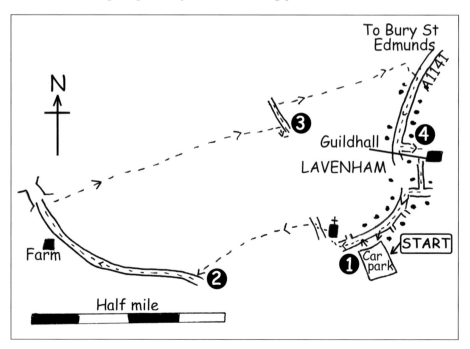

Spring I, who died in 1440, rose to be the premier merchant in the town, and during his lifetime and that of his son the town grew dramatically as more and more skilled workers, as well as merchants, moved in, building many fine timber-framed homes and workshops. Lavenham's prosperity reached its peak during the lifetime of Thomas Spring III, when a further influx of Flemish weavers fleeing persecution at home settled in the town. By the time Spring died in 1523 Lavenham was the fourteenth richest town in England, and paid more in taxes than London or York. Lavenham Blue was exported as far afield as Russia, Turkey and North Africa, as well as throughout Europe.

Nationwide economic depression in the 1620s hit Lavenham hard, and although it remained a centre for spinning throughout the 17th and 18th centuries, its glory days were over. The Industrial Revolution, which started in the textile industry, initially required water-powered machinery: water-rich Lancashire and Yorkshire flourished whilst Suffolk declined. However, this decline meant that Lavenham avoided the redevelopment caused by industrialization, and today remains the most perfect example of a medieval wool town in England.

THE WALK

❶ From the car park return to the main road. Cross over and turn left. In 50 yards turn right through the churchyard, and walk up to the church door.

The small Saxon church of St Peter & St Paul was completely rebuilt between 1485 and 1525 as the magnificent building we see today. The expense of the rebuilding was borne jointly by John de Vere, Earl of Oxford and lord of the manor of Lavenham, and Thomas Spring III, the town's richest merchant. The huge tower, 141 feet high, dominates the surrounding countryside. The magnificent porch, with its fan-vaulting and elaborate carving, is embellished with the shield and emblems (a star and a boar) of the de Veres. It is well worth looking inside the church, which has beautiful carved-wood screens, behind one of which is the elaborate tomb of Thomas Spring III, who died in 1523.

After visiting the church, descend steps by the tower into the lane and turn right. Go down the lane for 100 yards, then turn left over a stile beside a gate. Follow a broad track for 100 yards, and go through

The magnificent church of St Peter and St Paul, Lavenham, began life as a small Saxon church

the right-most of two gates. Keep straight on, with a hedge on your left. Keep ahead into a second field and keep straight on across the field to reach a lane.

❷ Turn right along the lane for ½ mile, ignoring a footpath off to the left. Pass the gates to a farm with a red pavilion at its gate and, 150 yards later, just before a bridge turn right onto a footpath. Follow the path, with a hedge on your left, for two-thirds of a mile, along two huge fields.

Look across the fields to your right to see how Lavenham church dominates the landscape. It offered immediate visual proof of the wealth of Lavenham and its patrons, Thomas Spring and John de Vere , to all the inhabitants in the vicinity and to all travellers through the countryside.

At the end of the second field, turn right onto an enclosed footpath. After 40 yards turn left onto a lane.

❸ Turn left along the lane for 80 yards and then turn right through a metal gate onto a path that follows the disused railway (a sign says 'Welcome to Lavenham Walk').

The railway was comparatively slow to reach Lavenham, not being opened until 1865 and then only as a spur line between Sudbury and Bury St Edmunds. This is further proof of the decline of Lavenham as a commercial centre by the 19th century. It was a single-track line, with a passing place at Lavenham station, and was opened initially as a goods service to carry sugar beet, one of Lavenham's major products at that time, to market. A passenger service was added later. The line closed in 1961.

Follow the path for 800 yards, ignoring side turns, eventually turning right to reach the main road. Turn right and walk along the main street of Lavenham.

Lavenham is one of the finest examples of a medieval wool town in England, with over 500 listed buildings. As the prosperity of the town grew, buildings of every size and shape were squeezed into any available space. Artisan families had their combined houses and workshops in the yards and alleys, whilst rich merchants built grand houses to display their wealth. There is little native stone in Suffolk suitable for building, and so timber was widely used. Much of the timber was pre-cut elsewhere, and then assembled in situ in a few days. Mortice and tenon joints, held in place with wooden spikes, kept the frame together, which was then infilled with wattle and daub. Weathering would mature the timbers to a light brown or grey colour. This walk goes along the main thoroughfares of Lavenham, which are lined with magnificent old buildings, but it is rewarding to spend time just wandering through the town's back streets.

❹ In ¼ mile, turn left along Market Lane to reach the Guildhall.

The Guildhall was built in 1528-9 by the Corpus Christi Guild, a religious organisation to which only the richest citizens of the town could belong. Throughout the Middle Ages religious guilds flourished, a link between the church and secular society. They provided a form of social security and welfare benefit for their members as well as providing spiritual support, prayers being said for departed members. By the 16th century there were over 500 such guilds in Suffolk, five in Lavenham alone, of which Corpus Christi was the wealthiest and most prestigious. The guild was suppressed 20 years later, at the time of the dissolution of the monasteries, and the Guildhall became the headquarters for the Guild of Merchant Clothiers, who oversaw every aspect of the cloth trade. The Guildhall was subsequently used as a prison, a workhouse, a shop and a warehouse.

The curious white colour of the Guildhall is the result of the timbers being washed with a solution of lime and water. The lime is sufficiently diluted that the timbers and carvings can be seen through it and the timber can breathe, but it is protected from weather and insects.

The Guildhall is open daily April to October from 11 am to 5 pm (closed Monday and Tuesday in April) and at weekends March and November from 11 am to 4 pm. There is an admission charge (free to National Trust members).

Across the square from the Guildhall stands the Little Hall, a 15th-century merchant's house originally built around a great hall but modernized and extended in the 16th century.

> **REFRESHMENTS**
>
> The Cock public house, next to the car park, is an old thatched building with a beer garden, offering a wide range of food and real ales. Telephone: 01787 247407.
>   There are numerous other pubs, tearooms and shops in Lavenham.

Go downhill, with the wall of the Guildhall on your left, and walk down Lady Street to Water Street.

Both Water Street and Shilling Street, which leads off it 100 yards down on the left, have numerous splendid old buildings. Here on the corner is the Wool Hall, built in 1464 by the religious guild of the Blessed Virgin (hence 'Lady Street') and later used for the buying and selling of wool. Next to this is the Swan Inn, which was built in 1400, the oldest of several inns that date from around that time.

Turn right past the Swan Inn to reach the main road, and then turn left up the main road to return to the car park.

WALK 11

FRAMLINGHAM CASTLE
WHO RULES AFTER HENRY VIII?
1553

Length: 4 miles

Framlingham Castle was built by Roger Bigod to a design first used by the Crusaders in the Holy Land

HOW TO GET THERE: Framlingham is just south of the A1120, at a junction of the B1119 and B1116 roads, 2 miles south of Dennington.

PARKING: The free car park next to Framlingham Castle, signposted from the approaches to town.

MAP: OS Landranger 156 (GR 285635).

INTRODUCTION

This walk from the historic town of Framlingham, goes down through the meadows that surround a lake, and then through pleasant countryside before returning to Framlingham Castle which is open to the public all year. The route uses field paths and quiet lanes, and affords good views of the castle. Walking is easy, and route-finding mostly straightforward, although in summer the path can sometimes be hard to detect in the crops.

THE HISTORICAL BACKGROUND

Framlingham Castle was home to Mary Tudor, daughter of Henry VIII, during the crucial days when her accession and perhaps even her life were at stake.

As death approached, Henry VIII issued a will outlining the succession to the throne. The crown would pass in the first instance to his young son Prince Edward; in the event of Edward's death without children, it would pass in turn to the prince's older sisters, first Mary and then Elizabeth; in the event of their deaths without children, it would pass to their nearest surviving relative, their cousin Lady Jane Grey.

King Henry died in January 1547 and his ten-year-old son acceded to the throne as Edward VI. A protector was appointed to help the child-king rule. For the first three years of the reign this was Edward's uncle, the Duke of Somerset, but in 1550 Somerset was ousted by his bitter rival, the ambitious John Dudley, Earl of Warwick, soon created Duke of Northumberland. The young king, unlike his father, was a zealous Protestant, and the tolerant approach to religion shown by Henry VIII was replaced by an increasingly harsh imposition of Protestantism. This dismayed the many Catholics in England, who blamed the Duke of Northumberland for their woes.

By 1553 it was becoming apparent that the king, who contracted tuberculosis, had not long to live. The position of the Duke of Northumberland looked precarious. Not only would Edward be succeeded by the Catholic Princess Mary, but the duke had alienated many non-Catholics with his greed and his arbitrary exercise of power. The duke therefore took a desperate gamble. He persuaded Edward to set aside his father's will and disinherit his sisters, on the grounds that both had been declared illegitimate by their father at various times. Instead, the crown would pass to Henry's fourth named heir, the 15-year-old Lady Jane Grey. In the meanwhile, the duke had arranged for Lady Jane to be married to his son, Lord Guildford Dudley.

Edward died on 6th July 1553, but news of this was kept quiet by Northumberland as he hurriedly prepared to proclaim Lady Jane as queen. Princess Mary was waiting at Framlingham Castle and, as

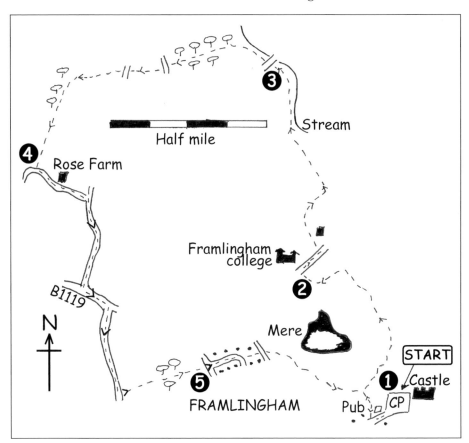

soon as news of the king's death reached her, she raised her banner and called on all loyal subjects to support her. The eastern counties rose in her favour, and within days 13,000 armed men had gathered at Framlingham. At the head of this army, Mary swept down to London to claim her rightful throne, and the nine-day rule of Lady Jane Grey was over.

THE WALK

❶ Leave the car park and turn right down the hill. Pass the Castle Inn and immediately turn right through a white kissing gate onto a footpath. Follow the footpath along the moat.

This is the moat that surrounds the outer bailey of Framlingham Castle. Framlingham is a very unusual design, in that whilst it has two baileys (courtyards), it has no separate keep. The outer bailey was surrounded by a moat and protective wall, whilst around the inner bailey was a strong curtain wall, 44 ft high, with 13 immensely strong towers. None of the towers were set into corners of the curtain wall, and thus provided a variety of angled sight-lines that commanded the whole of the wall's exterior. All the towers had wooden drawbridges leading onto the curtain wall, which enabled each tower to be isolated as a separate fortress. Unusually, the stairs leading down from the towers to the inner bailey were designed to favour defenders going down the stairwell rather than retreating up the stairs. Normally, the spiral staircase in towers would spiral clockwise, so that a right-handed defender retreating up the stairs would have free swing of his sword-arm, whilst a right-handed attacker following him up the stairs would find his sword-arm encumbered. At Framlingham, the spiral is anti-clockwise, the logic being that any invader would come over the curtain wall but could be enclosed in one isolated tower, which he would have to fight his way down. This design was first used by the Crusaders in the Holy Land, and copied here by Roger Bigod, Earl of Norfolk (see Walk 5), who built this castle between 1190 and 1210.

Leave the moat and keep downhill to a kissing gate. Go through the gate and turn right. Follow the path around the lake, called the Mere, and into trees.

The Mere is an artificial lake engineered by the lords of Framlingham Castle. This whole area to the west of the castle was initially a huge bog, which added to the protection of the castle by inhibiting approach from this side. The bog was drained and the Mere created, more for aesthetic than defensive reasons. In July 1553, when Queen Mary raised her standard on the walls of Framlingham, these meadows were the gathering ground for her loyal supporters. A total of 13,000 men camped here, surrounding the castle with an ever-increasing sea of tents and makeshift shelters, before marching on London. Never again was Queen Mary to see such an outpouring of popular support.

Ignore a footpath to the right going over a stile but follow the footpath to the left. Go through a kissing gate and immediately ignore a right turn but keep straight on, still circumnavigating the Mere. At the end of the enclosed footpath, cross a footbridge into a sports field and turn left. Walk along the edge of the sports field, to climb steps onto a drive.

'Bloody' Mary raised the royal standard at Framlingham in 1553, but reigned for just five years

❷ Turn right along the drive for 250 yards. Immediately past a drive leading to Framlingham College, turn left through a kissing gate.

Framlingham College is a public school, built in the mid 19th century with money left over from building the Albert Memorial in London.

Follow the hedge on your right and in 50 yards turn right with the hedge. Go uphill and in the top corner turn right. Go downhill along an enclosed footpath. Cross a footbridge and go through a pedestrian gate in front of buildings, and then turn left to a stile by a field gate. Cross the stile and turn right for 20 yards. In front of a field gate turn left at a finger-post. Follow the path across the centre of the field. A finger-post becomes apparent on the far side of the field. Cross a stile behind the finger-post and maintain the same direction along the next field, a stream close on your right.

❸ Follow the path out to a lane. Cross the lane and turn right, following the path around the side of a field, soon with the stream again on your right. Ignore a footbridge and finger-post on your right but continue around the field perimeter, to reach a track in the far corner. Follow the track through trees and out to a lane. Cross the lane and continue in the same direction along a field, the hedge close on your right, to reach a second lane.

Cross this lane also and maintain your direction across the next field, aiming for the middle of a row of trees opposite. At the trees turn left. Follow the field edge, the trees close on your right. Where the trees end keep ahead, following the boundary between two fields and soon passing a telephone pole. Keep ahead, now on a broad grassy strip, to pass to the left of trees, with farm buildings away to your left. Continue past more telephone poles to reach a lane.

❹   Turn left and follow the quiet lane past the pink farmhouse of Rose Farm. Follow the lane to a T-junction. Turn right and follow the lane for 500 yards to reach a main road. Turn left along the main road for 150 yards, and then turn right into New Street. Follow this lane for ¼ mile. About 100 yards after passing de-restricted speed signs, turn left at a finger-post. Cross the field by a broad path and enter woods. Follow the path through trees and across the next field to reach a road.

❺   Cross the road and keep straight on along Danforth Drive. At the far end of Danforth Drive, keep ahead along an enclosed footpath, to the left of a bungalow (No 53). At the end of the footpath, cross the road to a kissing gate and go half-right down the grassy slope. Go through the hedge over a footbridge and bear left down to green metal gates.

The relationship of Mere to Castle can be seen to its best from here. When the Mere was created, it was not for defensive purposes. Indeed, the bog that was here before provided better defence. Instead, the Mere was created to provide an aesthetic foreground to the castle, giving it a fairy-tale appearance that emphasized its grandeur and thus provided a strong visual reminder of the power of the Dukes of Norfolk.

Cross the drive and enter the meadow that surrounds the Mere. Turn right and follow the path through a kissing gate beside a wooden field gate. Maintain your direction to a second kissing gate. Do NOT go through this gate but instead turn left and follow the fence to a footbridge. Cross the bridge and keep ahead, ignoring a turn to the right, to reach a kissing gate beside a field gate. Go through the gate and keep ahead for 5 yards to go through another kissing gate on your right. Follow the path uphill, soon reaching the moat. Keep ahead to return to the Castle Inn, castle and car park.

To visit the castle, keep ahead to the ticket office in the gatehouse.

Framlingham has always been the most important castle in Suffolk, and has seen many episodes that display the touchy relationship between the

Earls and Dukes of Norfolk and the Crown.

The first Norman castle was built on the site of a Saxon fort by Roger Bigod, whose son Hugh was created Earl of Norfolk by King Stephen. Hugh rebelled unsuccessfully against Henry II in 1173 (see Walk 5) and was forced to surrender Framlingham Castle, which was dismantled. The site was returned to Hugh's son, Roger, in 1189, who built the present castle. Roger was to rebel against his King, John, in 1215.

The Bigod line died out in 1312 and the castle and earldom passed to the Mowbray family. The Mowbrays continued the tradition when Thomas Mowbray, first Duke of Norfolk, rebelled against King Richard II in 1399 and was banished. His son, also Thomas, was executed for rebelling against the next king, Henry IV, in 1405.

In 1476 the castle and dukedom passed to the Howard family. The first Howard duke died at Bosworth fighting for Richard III and his son spent much of the next reign, of Henry VII, imprisoned in the Tower, before being released and becoming a loyal supporter of Henry VIII. The next duke, who tried to cement his position by marrying his niece Catherine Howard to the king, was also imprisoned in the Tower by Henry VIII. Framlingham was seized by the king and became the eventual home of his daughter, Princess Mary, and the base from which she launched her claim for the throne.

Although Queen Mary restored the staunchly Catholic Howards to their lands, the saga of rebellion continued, with the next duke being executed by Queen Elizabeth for his support of the Catholic Mary Queen of Scots, and Framlingham again being seized by the Crown. It was restored to the Howards by James I, by which time the family fortunes were becoming centred on their lands around Arundel in Sussex, and Framlingham Castle passed out of history.

Framlingham castle is open all year, from 10 am to 6 pm, April to September; 10 am to 5 pm in October; 10 am to 4 pm November to March. There is an entrance charge (free to members of English Heritage).

WALK 12
HOLKHAM HALL
THE REVOLUTION IN AGRICULTURE 1776

Length: 5 miles

Holkham Hall was completed around 1764 and contains many treasures

HOW TO GET THERE:	**PARKING:** Use the car park at	**MAP:** OS Landranger 132
Holkham Gap, from where the walk begins, is reached along a private road leading north from the A149, 1 mile west of Wells-next-the-Sea, opposite the entrance to Holkham Estate.	Holkham Gap (fee payable).	(GR 891448).

INTRODUCTION

This walk takes you through the woods and deer park of Holkham Estate, passing magnificent Holkham Hall and the imposing monument to Thomas Coke. It then crosses reclaimed coastal land

and passes through tree-covered sand dunes before returning along the wonderful sands of Holkham Bay. The walk uses mainly tracks and the beach, the terrain being flat and gentle underfoot.

THE HISTORICAL BACKGROUND

Towards the end of the 18th century, the process of farming in Britain was revolutionised. One of the men at the forefront of this Agricultural Revolution was the owner of Holkham Hall, 'Coke of Norfolk', Thomas William Coke.

For 30 years, from 1720 until 1750, there had been a severe depression in agriculture. The prices paid for agricultural produce fell, leading to widespread hardship amongst farming communities. Many small farmers, scratching out a living by selling their surplus produce, had even that meagre income disappear, whilst the wages of those who worked for others were cut. Many of the poorest members of rural communities left the land to seek better fortunes in the nearby towns. Bigger landlords fared better. Not only did they have more wealth behind them, which enabled them to weather the depression, but they were able to increase their estates by buying up cheaply the land of their poorer, dispossessed neighbours, and by enclosing previously common land.

Larger estates enabled some landlords to experiment with advanced farming techniques that had been impossible when the land was packaged between a multitude of small holdings. Thomas William Coke of Holkham was the most successful farmer of his day. Fascinated by farming, he set about developing his lands in a controlled, scientific manner, carefully recording and publishing his efforts, his successes and his failures. He vastly improved the quality of the soil on his estates by mixing sand and marl into it. To prevent soil exhaustion, he rotated crops on a systematic basis, and experimented by adding turnips, clover and new grasses to the mix. He turned to producing grain and raising cattle rather than sheep. Coke also gave his tenants unprecedented long leases on their farms, to encourage them to sink their own money into improving their farms. Coke regularly published the results of his efforts, and had annual 'fairs' on his estates, the forerunner of today's agricultural shows, where visitors in their thousands could see and learn from his experiments.

The 'Norfolk System' that Coke introduced transformed the face of English farming, enabling food to be produced more plentifully than

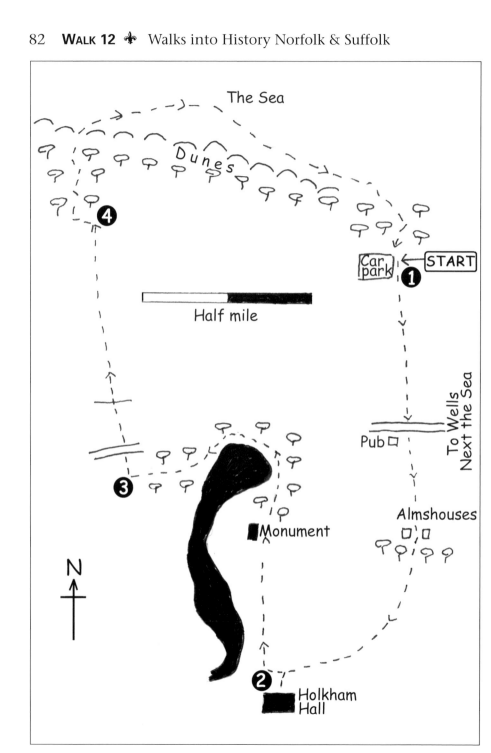

ever before, food that was essential to feed the ever-growing urban population in Britain's industrial cities. Thomas Coke was a key figure in the Agricultural Revolution, without which the Industrial Revolution could not have occurred.

THE WALK

❶   From the car park walk back along the drive to the main road. Cross the road and continue ahead up the estate road, passing the Victoria public house on your right, with the tearooms and toilets just to your left.

Thomas Coke had a very paternal attitude to his tenants, building cottages and community buildings for them. This philosophy was continued by later owners of the estate. Note the war memorial as you pass, commemorating men from the Holkham Estate who died in the two world wars.

Continue along the drive for ¼ mile, to pass between almshouses and through gates into the deer park.

The almshouses were built in 1757 by Lady Margaret Dufton, wife to the first Thomas Coke and aunt of Thomas William, who ran the estate after her husband's death and carried on his building works. Lady Margaret used money left to her by her father, the Earl of Thanet, to build almshouses for three men and three women of the estate, who were unable otherwise to support themselves.

Keep ahead along the drive for ½ mile as it winds through the deer park to reach Holkham Hall.

The estate at Holkham had been occupied by the Coke family since 1609, when the manor was purchased by Sir Edward Coke, Attorney-General to both Queen Elizabeth and James I, who is believed to have originated the phrase 'an Englishman's home is his castle'. The present hall and formal park were not there in Sir Edward's day. Instead, he lived here in an elaborate Elizabethan manor house, known as Hill Hall, surrounded by a walled deer park.

   Sir Edward's grandson, Thomas Coke, 1st Earl of Leicester, inherited the estate when he was only ten years old. For the good of his education, he was sent at the age of fifteen on a Grand Tour of Europe, where he fell in love with Italy and its classical architecture. The tour lasted for six years.

On his return, aged 21, he married Lady Margaret Tufton and set about converting Hill Hall into a splendid house in the Neo-classical or Palladian style.

Designs for Holkham Hall were drawn up by Coke and his friend William Kent, and the architect Matthew Brettingham was employed to turn them into reality. The first foundations were dug in 1734 and building went on for 30 years until the present magnificent hall was finished. Thomas Coke died in 1759, before building was completed, and it was left to his wife, Lady Margaret, to finish the work.

After Lady Margaret died in 1775, the Hall passed to her nephew and, on his death a year later, to his son, Thomas William Coke. It was this Coke who was to devote his life to farming. He also employed the landscape architect Capability Brown to design the formal park that surrounds the hall, creating the lake from a tidal creek and planting thousands of Mediterranean evergreen oaks.

Holkham Hall contains many treasures. A Statue Gallery houses the collection of Roman antiquities brought back by the first Thomas Coke from his Grand Tour, as well as a good art collection, and the Marble Hall is the finest Palladian hall in the country.

The Hall is open between June and September, Thursdays to Mondays, 1 pm until 5 pm. It is also open bank holidays. There is an admission charge.

❷   With your back to the Hall, and the lake on your left, walk ahead slightly uphill to the monument.

The huge monument was erected to commemorate Thomas William Coke, who devoted his life to farming. In 1776, when Coke was 22, he inherited Holkham Estate, then worth £2,000 a year. Such were the improvements he made that when he died in 1842 it was worth £20,000. Coke was MP for Norfolk for 50 years, but because there were two other Cokes in the House of Commons, he was always addressed as 'Coke of Norfolk', and the nickname stuck. In 1837, at the age of 83, he was elevated to the peerage and took the family title, Earl of Leicester.

On the four plinths on the corners of the monument are represented a bull, a sheep and two ploughs, including the Rotherham plough, a revolutionary design that Coke popularised by using it to great effect at Holkham and which was to help transform farming methods. On the sides of the plinth are bas-reliefs showing sheep shearing and other farming activities, commemorating the huge Holkham sheep shearings. These were the fairs Coke held annually at Holkham, at which he showed his innovations off to hundreds of neighbours and thereby propagated his new ideas.

From the monument maintain your direction along a grassy track. Follow the track as it winds through trees, going gently downhill to reach the lake.

Until the late 1600s this lake was a tidal creek, connected via saltmarshes to the sea a mile to the north. Vikings sailed up this creek to build a town at Holkham ('Holk' meaning 'ship' and 'ham' meaning 'town'). This creek was dammed by Capability Brown to create the lake seen today.

Join a clear semi-surfaced track and bear left, following the track around the lake. Follow the track through gates, leaving the lake and climbing gently through trees.

Thomas Coke planted thousands of trees in Holkham Park, to act as windbreaks. Much of the western end of the park was devoted to agriculture, and still is today.

❸ Follow the track to a T-junction and turn right down to monumental gates. Pass through the gates and cross the road to a gate opposite. Cross a stile beside the gate and keep ahead down a grassy track.

The road you just crossed marks the line of the coast prior to 1639. From Roman times onwards, the sea levels around England rose. Much of the low-lying coastal plain of Norfolk was flooded with increasing regularity, and previously fertile farmland turned into saltmarsh. At the end of the Roman era, AD 400, this was the coast. A line of shingle spits and sand dunes ran parallel to the shore, where the trees can be seen ahead in the distance. Between these two was an area of saltmarsh and tidal inlets.

At a cross track, keep ahead. Follow the broad track for ¼ mile. Where the track bends right and then left, at metal gates on your left, look into the field on your left to see the remains of an Iron Age fort.

In the Iron Age, from 700 BC until the arrival of the Romans, this area was the land of the Iceni tribe (see Walk 2). After the Romans landed in Britain, the Iceni felt threatened and built forts consisting of earth banks topped by wooden palisades to protect their scattered communities. The embankments of Holkham fort, built around AD 47, can still be seen today. Nearby is a concrete Second World War pillbox, a reminder of a later conflict.

Continue along the track for another ¼ mile to enter woods.

From around 1639 onwards efforts were made to reclaim the salt marshes and Thomas Coke was especially active in this area. Large stands of pines were planted to stabilize the coastal sand dunes, which were raised to provide protection from the sea. The land reclaimed was improved by the addition of sand and marls, crops were planted scientifically to feed the soil, and gradually arable farmland was created again.

❹   Just inside the woods, at a cross track, keep straight on. The track soon narrows to a sandy path and climbs. Follow the main path as it undulates through woods.

You are walking through stands of Corsican pines planted specifically to stabilize the coastal sand dunes. Pines, which have shallow roots and like sandy soil, are ideally suited for this task.

At the end of the trees maintain the same direction through the dunes to reach the foreshore. Turn right and walk along the beach, keeping parallel to the dunes and curving right to keep the trees on your right. Walk between dunes, keeping a constant distance from the trees. Soon there is a tidal lagoon on your left: curve constantly rightwards, with the dunes close on your right. Where the higher dunes end, keep ahead along the edge of a salt marsh, trees now in front of you. At the inland end of the marsh, trees now close on your right, keep ahead, soon with a picket fence on your right. Half-way along the fence, turn right up a path to an observation platform with bench. Keep ahead along a duck-boarded path to return to the car park.

WALK 13
HUNSTANTON
FIVE HUNDRED YEARS
OF SMUGGLING

Length: 4 miles

Hunstanton's famous 'striped' cliffs are the tallest in Norfolk

HOW TO GET THERE:
Hunstanton is on the A149,
18 miles north of Kings Lynn.

PARKING: In the pay-and-
display car park on the north
cliffs at Hunstanton. The car
park is clearly signed from the
A149.

MAP: OS Landranger 132
(GR 676420).

INTRODUCTION

This walk starts on the spectacular cliffs of Hunstanton, goes through
the pretty seaside town and then out into the surrounding
countryside, along tracks and quiet lanes before returning to the vast
sandy beach north of the town. Walking is easy and there are no
significant gradients.

THE HISTORICAL BACKGROUND

Today, Hunstanton relies upon the tourist trade for much of its prosperity but, for many centuries, a large part of its income came from an altogether darker trade, smuggling. Interestingly, the trade started, not to smuggle contraband into England, but out of it.

Technically, smuggling is the movement across a border of goods that will be taxed, or banned or confiscated. When trade is not regulated, smuggling does not really exist. Until the 12th century England was largely self-sufficient, and cross-border trade so insignificant that it did not attract the attention of the Crown. This altered in the 13th century. The production of wool became a major industry, and English wool was highly prized by the textile manufacturers of Flanders and Holland. By 1275 30,000 sacks of wool a year were being exported. Edward I, financially stretched, saw a potentially lucrative source of income, and in 1275 imposed export duties on wool leaving England. Since coastal trade is conspicuous, it was far easier to tax wool as it left the country rather than on the farms where it was produced, and so customs staff, or excisemen, were employed at ports such as Kings Lynn to intercept exports and levy a duty upon them.

Wool merchants naturally resented the erosion of their profit margin by taxation, and so looked for ways of avoiding the duty. Since the ports were watched by Crown officials, the merchants took to shipping their wool abroad from secluded beaches, safe from the prying eyes of the excisemen. Hunstanton, with its broad flat beaches on a remote stretch of coast and an easy sea crossing away from Holland, was an ideal embarkation point for the wool smugglers. Not that the merchants engaged in smuggling themselves. Rather, they sold their wool to middlemen who then set up a distribution chain of freelance hauliers and sailors to convey the wool abroad. Naturally, these entrepreneurs soon realized that it was unprofitable to have their boats return from the continent empty, so brought back luxury goods such as wine, which could be sold at a good profit in England.

Successive monarchs, embroiled in continental wars, taxed an ever greater range of goods. Increasingly, as prosperity increased in England, so too did the demand for luxuries such as wines and spirits, silks and chocolate, later tea and tobacco. All these were subject to increasing levels of import tax by a Crown stretched for cash and this, in turn, increased the opportunities for smuggling until by the end of the 18th century smuggling was a major part of the economy of coastal towns like Hunstanton.

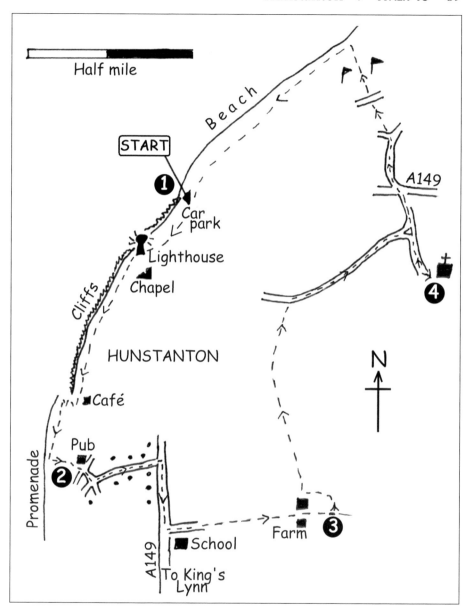

THE WALK

❶ From the car park walk along the cliff, the sea on your right, passing the lighthouse and the ruins of St Edmund's Chapel.

The lighthouse, now disused, was built in the 19th century as a navigational aid, but for centuries smugglers had used this headland, the highest point on the coast for many miles. They would place lanterns or signal beacons here to guide smuggling vessels to the beaches north and south, where accomplices would be waiting to unload contraband.

The small St Edmund's chapel was built in Saxon times, and the stone arch dates from that era.

Follow the broad green track along the top of the cliffs for ½ mile to reach a cliff-top café. From the café descend a ramp to the seafront promenade. Turn right for a few yards to view the cliffs.

Hunstanton is famous for its striped cliffs, 60 feet high and the tallest cliffs in Norfolk. Alternate bands of rock, all sandstones formed by deposits on the beds of prehistoric oceans in different eras, give them their distinctive colour. The oldest, bottom, layer is a sandstone called carstone, common in Norfolk; above that is a band of rare red chalk, whilst above that is the youngest layer of rock, a white chalk.

Walk along the promenade for 250 yards. Just before the kiosks, turn up an access road to regain the cliff top by the Golden Lion Hotel.

You are now in the centre of Victorian Hunstanton. Prior to the 19th-century tourist boom there were hardly any buildings here (the major settlement was Old Hunstanton, behind the dunes a mile to the north) and where the promenade now runs were miles of empty beach, ideal for smugglers to land their illicit cargo.

❷   Pass in front of the Golden Lion and the Tourist Information Office, and then cross half-right over the road. Go along the road opposite, passing the Princess Theatre on your right. Keep along the road to reach a cross road with Westgate, the Union church opposite you. Turn left up Westgate and follow the road to reach the main road (Kings Lynn Road). Turn right for 500 yards to reach pedestrian traffic lights. Cross at the lights and turn into Downs Road just to your left. Follow the road past the school and keep ahead along a track. Follow the track to pass between the buildings of Lodge Farm.

❸   Some 100 yards past the farm, turn left onto a rough track along the edge of a field. Soon turn sharp left to follow the perimeter of

The beaches at Hunstanton provided a regular landing point for smugglers

Lodge Farm. The track soon turns right again. Follow this straight green track slightly uphill.

The Peddars Way is a long-distance route that has been in use since the Iron Age, connecting inland East Anglia to the coast at Old Hunstanton, where ferries could cross the Wash to modern Lincolnshire as well as serving as an anchorage for shipping from the Continent. In the 17th and 18th centuries this track was known as the Smugglers Way, and the illicit traffic along it was huge. To give one example: in the last six months of 1745, 4,550 horses, carrying over 340 tons of contraband and accompanied by huge bands of horse handlers, porters and guards, passed along the Smugglers Way.

Naturally, this amount of traffic attracted a great deal of interest, and local superstitions were played upon to discourage too much close attention. One story persistent in local legend is the tale of Old Shuck, a ghost dog with one blazing fiery eye, whom to look upon is certain death. Smugglers turned this tale to advantage by tying a lantern to the neck of a black ram and sending it running down the lanes when a convoy was due, to scare superstitious locals safely indoors.

More prosaically, there was a strong financial benefit for villagers to turn a blind eye to smuggling activities. Many of the local population lived at barely subsistence level. A week's backbreaking work in the fields, for those who could even find work, would earn seven shillings. The same could be earned in a single night unloading for the smugglers, or 'moonlighting' as it was called. A sizeable proportion of villagers in the tight-knit communities of Norfolk received a handsome supplement to their incomes in this way, deterring them from calling adverse attention to the smugglers' activities.

The trees, seen off to the right, mark the boundary of Hunstanton Hall, home to local landowners the Le Strange family. Many local gentry throughout Norfolk profited from the smuggling trade, either actively, by investing money in illicit ventures or by buying luxury goods at knock-down prices, or tacitly, simply by keeping quiet about an activity that provided widespread unofficial employment for their tenants.

Follow the green track out to a lane and turn right. Follow the quiet lane for 800 yards to reach a T-junction, a small green with a tree and seat in its centre. Turn right past the duck pond to reach the church.

Responsibility for suppressing smuggling along the north-east coast of Norfolk lay with customs officials based in Kings Lynn, and with very limited manpower they had a nearly impossible job in the face of local non-cooperation. A poignant example of this can be seen in the graveyard of the 14th-century church of St Mary the Virgin. In September 1784 customs officials, supported by a troop of mounted dragoons, intercepted a large party of smugglers unloading their cargo on the nearby beach. The heavily armed smugglers opened fire: William Webb, a dragoon, died immediately; a customs official, William Green, was mortally wounded and died the following day. The graves of both men can be seen close to the south porch of the church here. Two smugglers were arrested for the murders. Despite incontrovertible evidence against them, such was the sympathy felt for smuggling that both men were acquitted by a local jury. A retrial was demanded, and again a 'not guilty' verdict resulted. In the face of such blatant disregard of the law, it is hardly surprising that smuggling flourished.

A hedged enclosure on the far, northern, side of the church houses the tombs of the Le Strange family, whose family seat, Hunstanton Hall, is next to the church.

❹   After viewing the churchyard, return to the green and keep ahead along the lane to reach the main road. Cross the road with care into Waterworks Road opposite. Follow this road for 400 yards, and then turn left into Wodehouse Road. Immediately bear right onto a gravel track, Smugglers Lane.

As its name implies, this trackway was regularly used by smugglers to bring their contraband from the beach, on the first stage of its journey inland along the Peddars Way.

Follow the enclosed track, soon narrowing into a grassy footpath. Cross a road and keep ahead along the enclosed footpath to reach the access road for a golf course. Keep ahead on a clear sandy path across the golf course. On the far side of the fairways keep ahead on a clear path between beach chalets to reach the beach.

Before Hunstanton expanded in the 19th century, the north beach was not overlooked by any housing, and this vast expanse of sand was a regular landing point for smugglers. Local seamen supplemented their income by guiding smuggling vessels through the sandbanks to this deserted beach, where labourers from Old Hunstanton were paid handsomely for a few hours' work unloading the cargo and reloading it into wagons and onto pack mules for its journey south.

Turn left along the beach and walk back to the car park on the cliffs ahead of you, eventually bearing left to find the path leading to the cliff-top.

WALK 14
FELIXSTOWE FERRY
MARTELLO TOWERS AND THE
THREAT FROM NAPOLEON 1805

Length: 7 miles

The coastal defences known as Martello Towers were named after a stone tower at Mortella on Corsica

HOW TO GET THERE:	**PARKING:** In the pay & display	**MAP:** OS Landranger169
Felixstowe Ferry is at the end of the road leading north from Felixstowe.	car park at Felixstowe Ferry.	(GR 329377).

INTRODUCTION

Although this walk is quite long, it is very easy underfoot. It starts along the banks of the River Deben and the King's Fleet, a landscape any invading Napoleonic army would have encountered. It then crosses fields, climbing gently to give beautiful views over the river valley. It returns to the coast for a final exhilarating stroll along the sea-wall, passing two fine examples of Martello towers.

THE HISTORICAL BACKGROUND

On the coast near Felixstowe Ferry stand two Martello towers, witness to the threat of invasion posed to this country in the early 19th century by Napoleon.

In 1802 the Peace Treaty of Amiens ended nine years of war between Britain and revolutionary France. This was only a temporary respite, for 14 months later the war resumed. This time France was led by a far more formidable enemy, Napoleon Bonaparte, whose primary war aim for the next two years was the invasion of England.

Napoleon's obvious invasion route was the short sea crossing from the Pas de Calais to the beaches of Kent, Essex or Suffolk. Here wide beaches were backed by flat fields, ideal countryside for the highly manoeuvrable French army, and London was only a short march away. Although the first line of defence was the English Navy, there was always the danger that the French fleet would manage to secure the Channel for 24 hours, which was all the time that would be necessary for an invasion armada to land Napoleon's *Grande Armée* on England's shores. Protection of many miles of exposed beaches became of paramount importance, with only limited funds available for the task.

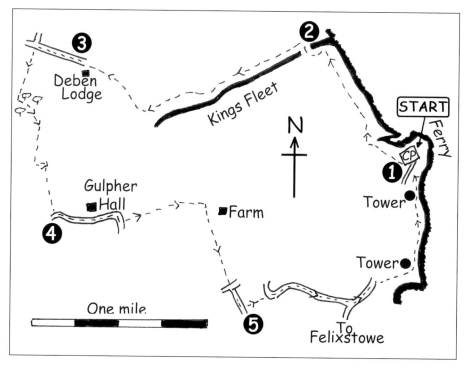

The solution was the Martello tower, a string of brick-built gun-platform cum watch towers built in close proximity to each other all along the coast, providing mutual reinforcement and interlocking fields of fire. No single tower was strong enough to withstand prolonged naval bombardment, but they could repel assault by infantry, and their sheer numbers would ensure devastating firepower against any landing force. The towers would make landings costly in terms of casualties, and just as important, the need to suppress them would buy valuable time for more defenders to arrive from the garrisons around Ipswich and Harwich, and prepare to meet the invaders in the flat, marshy countryside behind the beaches.

THE WALK

❶   Go to the landward end of the car park, away from the ferry and café, and turn right onto the embankment at a finger-post.

There was a ferry across the Deben estuary in the early 19th century, but by then the river was too silted up to have provided a channel for an invading fleet to penetrate inland. It was anticipated that any invaders would land on the wide beaches to the south of here (where Martello towers were built for defence) and then march inland, aiming initially to the great port of Harwich and beyond that, to London. Today the land is farmland, reclaimed from the sea, but in the 19th century it would have been much boggier, a marshland criss-crossed with water channels.

Walk along the embankment (flood defences for the River Deben) as it follows the riverbank. Cross a stile and turn left with the embankment. Follow the embankment as it zigzags across the neck of a water channel, before descending steps on your left.

❷   Continue ahead, water now on your left.

This stretch of water is called the King's Fleet. Originally it opened into the River Deben and thence into the open sea, and it was here that in 1338 King Edward III assembled a fleet of over 100 ships to carry his army to invade France at the start of the Hundred Years War. Nearly five centuries later it would have served a very different function: to defend England from invasion by the French. If the Napoleonic armies had succeeded in landing on the beaches south of the Deben estuary, the King's Fleet would have

William Pitt the Younger, Prime Minister from 1759–1806, ordered the building of 103 Martello Towers as a defence against invasion

been the first natural barrier they encountered as they marched inland. The great strength of the Napoleonic army was its ability to combine the three wings of infantry, cavalry and artillery into one devastating combined attack. The watery channels across this flat landscape such as King's Fleet would have provided ideal defensive moats. Defenders on the northern side would be protected from frontal attack, and could break up any combined attack trying to cross under fire. The waterway would stop cavalry and artillery from crossing and any infantry who swam the canal would not arrive on the far side with dry powder, and thus fall easy prey to the waiting British.

Follow the gravel track along the side of the King's Fleet for 1 mile, then turn right with the track, away from the Fleet. Follow the track for a further ½ mile, until it becomes a tarmac lane at Deben Lodge.

❸ Continue along the tarmac lane for ¼ mile. Opposite where a lane joins from the right, turn left at a finger-post and follow a path across a field. At a line of bushes on the skyline, go through a gap in the hedge at a waymark post. Continue in the same direction down the next field. At the bottom of the slope, turn left onto a wide footpath into trees. Follow the path, soon narrowing, through a strip of woodland and then continue on a clear path to a stile. Cross the stile and continue across the field, aiming for the left end of a line of trees opposite. At the trees, go half right, with the fence close on your right. In the top corner of the field. cross a stile and then a footbridge. Keep ahead, aiming between two trees seen in the mid-distance. At the trees, turn left in the corner of the field and follow the field boundary towards a wood. Just before the woods, turn right at a waymark-post and follow a grassy track towards a house on the skyline. Follow a track, surfaced after the house, to join a lane at another house.

❹   Maintain your direction along the lane, passing Gulpher Hall. Some 200 yards past the Hall turn sharp right with the lane, at a house named 'The Brook'. In another 10 yards turn left into a field (a finger-post is in the hedge on the left, all but hidden). Go up a faint grassy path between two fields. Once over the skyline, keep ahead, aiming for a telegraph pole in front of the wood opposite, and eventually meeting a hedge on your left. Follow the hedge as it bears right. Keep ahead passing farm buildings away to the left. Continue to follow the path, initially with the fence close on your left, towards houses ahead. Go through a barrier onto a road. Cross the road and continue along Ferry Road opposite.

❺   Just before the first house on the left, turn left at a finger-post across a field. On reaching a lane maintain your direction. Follow the lane for ½ mile to reach a main road. Cross the road and turn left for 100 yards. Where the green link fence on the left ends, bear right at a finger-post and follow a line of waymark posts across the golf course to reach the sea wall. Turn left along the sea wall, soon passing the first Martello tower.

In 1804-5 a line of towers was built along the shoreline of England, mostly along the coast from Portsmouth to Folkestone. These were called Martello towers, named after a stone-built tower at Mortella on Corsica. Circular fortified towers had fallen out of fashion by the 16th century, when the invention of gunpowder made them vulnerable to bombardment, but when Mortella Tower was occupied by pirates and they subsequently held out for two days against the Royal Navy, this wisdom was reassessed.

Almost every Martello tower had the same design (the exception to this being the most northerly tower, just south of Aldeburgh, which is a far more elaborate structure). They were 33 feet tall, with walls between 13 feet wide at the base to 6 feet wide at parapet level, and slightly elliptical in shape, with the thickest part of the walls to seaward. They were built of brick, and strengthened with lime mortar to withstand bombardment. Entrance was at first floor level, on the landward side, and there was accommodation for a garrison of 24 men and one officer. Slit windows enabled the beach to be raked with musket fire. On the flat roof of each tower was a gun capable of traversing 360 degrees. This could fire either a

REFRESHMENTS

At Felixstowe Ferry are the Victoria Inn (tel. 01394 271636) and the Ferry Boat Inn (tel. 01394 284203). Both have outdoor seating and offer a range of food and beers.
There is also a café.

24-pound cannon ball 1,000 yards, which would have caused immense damage to lightly-built landing craft approaching the beaches: or it could fire grape-shot, a canister which would spray between 84 and 232 musket balls up to 350 yards, with devastating effect upon infantry. The towers were built to be 700 to 1,000 yards apart, so that they could command the whole beach with interlocking cannon fire.

The towers were cheap and quick to build, and in total 103 were built at the instruction of Prime Minister Pitt the Younger. The destruction of the French and Spanish navies at Trafalgar in 1805 removed the threat of invasion, and the towers never saw active service. Many were allowed to fall into disrepair during the 19th century, and some were used for naval target practice and destroyed. In 1940 the surviving towers were repaired and put on a war footing again in the face of threatened German invasion.

Follow the sea wall for ¼ mile to pass the second tower. Continue along the wall to reach Felixstowe Ferry and the end of the walk.

Elmsett and the Tithe War of 1932

Length: 3½ or 2 miles

The monument at Elmsett remembers the 'tithe war' of 1932

HOW TO GET THERE: Elmsett is 4 miles north-east of Hadleigh, in a network of minor roads north of the A1071 Hadleigh to Ipswich road..

PARKING: There is plenty of roadside parking in the centre of village, near the shop and pub, but please park with consideration for residents.

MAP: OS Landranger 155 (GR 055466).

INTRODUCTION

This walk starts in the quiet village of Elmsett and visits places connected with the Tithe War. It follows field paths and quiet lanes that afford superb views over the gently rolling countryside. Walking is mostly easy, although the stretch from Rhoods Farm back to Elmsett is overgrown in places and poorly marked, and contains one brief strenuous section. This part of the walk can be avoided by using the shorter route.

THE HISTORICAL BACKGROUND

Today Elmsett is a sleepy village in the heart of the Suffolk countryside, but in 1932 it was at the centre of a fierce controversy known as the Tithe War.

From Norman times onwards, a tax called a tithe had been levied in order to support the Church. This tithe was one tenth of all the produce of the countryside, and it was originally paid in kind – a tenth of all crops, one in ten of all livestock born. This was specifically to support clergymen, who were not paid a cash wage for doing full-time pastoral work, but still needed to eat. After the Reformation, this tithe was continued to support the Church of England. Even though with time the Church lost its central role in society, it continued to collect the tithe. In 1836, an Act of Parliament converted the tithe to a cash payment, the tithe rent-charge. This was only paid on agricultural produce, and since farming was now only one part of the economy, the tithe was increasingly resented within the farming community.

The Industrial Revolution and the ensuing growth of cities greatly increased demand for food, and the farming community prospered throughout the 19th and early 20th centuries. In 1880 average farm wages in Suffolk were 15 shillings a week: by the end of the First World War they had risen to 40 shillings. But then, in 1921, in the face of cheap imports of food from abroad, the price of agricultural produce collapsed. Home-grown wheat and beef, the two main products of Suffolk, halved in price. Farm wages collapsed almost overnight, to 25 shillings for a 52-hour week. This was the start of a depression in farming that was to last for the next 15 years.

Elmsett was a typical farming community in Suffolk. Most able-bodied men worked on the land, living, in the main, in tied cottages. Many farmers were tenants, working land they did not own but only rented. As the Agricultural Depression continued, farmers were

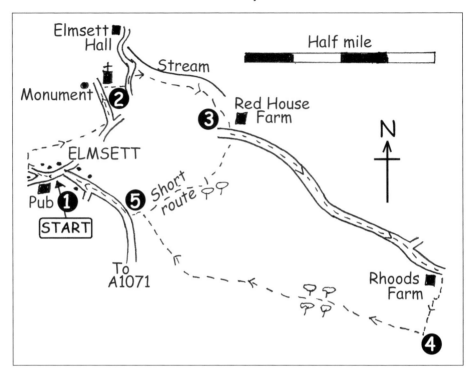

plunged into debt, and many went bankrupt. Regardless of the farmers' hardship, the Church of England refused to forego its tithe rent-charge, which was fixed to the pre-war price of corn not to the current price. For many farmers, sheer poverty made it impossible to pay the tithe. The Church responded by threatening to confiscate goods in lieu of payment. In 1931 the Suffolk Tithepayers Association was formed, to support all farmers who refused to pay the tithe. In May 1932, Charles Westren of Elmsett refused to pay his tithe and the Tithe War was underway.

THE WALK
❶ With the pub and village store on your left, walk along the road, bearing right with the main road in 50 yards. In 100 yards, turn right into a gravel drive along the side of the village green. Follow the drive to the gates of the Old Rectory.

The rectory was originally Church property, owned to provide a home for the clergyman who looked after the parish of Elmsett and officiated at the church, visible across the fields. It was to support such clergymen that the tithe was introduced. The rector in 1932 played no part in the controversy surrounding Charles Westren's refusal to pay the tithe.

Go through a field gate to the left of the rectory gates and keep ahead along the side of a field, with a hedge close on your right. Follow the path along the edge of a second field, crossing a plank bridge and continuing along a third field to reach a lane. Maintain the same direction along the side of the lane to reach a side turning. Turn left along this lane to reach the church.

By May 1932, local farmer Charles Westren owed £127 in unpaid tithes. His offer to pay off £12 a month, all he could afford, was refused, and the Church authorities decided to seize assets in compensation. On 2nd May 'The commissioners of Queen Anne's Bounty', effectively bailiffs acting on behalf of the Church, were sent to impound eight cornstacks, valued at £385, which could be auctioned to clear the debt. The seizure was intended to be a surprise raid, but as no local hauliers would take part, lorries had to be hired from as far away as Cambridge. The result was that locals had plenty of notice of the raid, and prepared to repel it. We shall tell that story in a moment.

The monument to the left was erected by the Westren family to commemorate the events of May 1932. It shows certain poetic licence, talking, for instance, of the seizure of a 'baby's bed and blankets', which didn't actually occur. It is nevertheless a potent memorial to the strong feelings evoked by this episode.

❷   Turn right and go through the churchyard, passing the church on your left, and follow the path to a drive. Keep straight on, passing Church Farm to reach a lane.

Church Farm was one of two farmed by Charles Westren. His main farm, and the target of the raid on 2nd May 1932, was Elmsett Hall ¼ mile up the lane to the left. When the lorries of the bailiffs came along this lane at 6.30 am, the bells of the church were rung to alert villagers. News was rapidly sent by telephone and word of mouth, and shortly a crowd of over 300 gathered in this lane to prevent the bailiffs' lorries from leaving. In the face of such popular hostility, and unable to successfully enter Elmsett Hall, the bailiffs rapidly left with only a third of one haystack on their lorries, instead of the eight stacks they had come for. They retreated down this lane, past a cheering crowd, with the church bells again ringing to celebrate the villagers' triumph.

Turn left down the lane for 100 yards. Where the lane bends left, turn right at a finger-post. To see Elmsett Hall, walk up the lane for another 300 yards: it is on your left.

When the bailiffs arrived early on the morning of 2nd May, the church bells already ringing in their ears as the alarm was sounded, they found Elmsett Hall effectively barricaded. Wagons had been placed over the track leading to the farm, elm trees had been cut down and laid across the drive, a chicken house had been dragged across the drive near the house, and a trench had been dug across the gateway, on the pretext of inspecting an underground pipe. Charles Westren stood at his farm, holding a large bull on a rein. The lorry drivers made no attempt to enter the Hall, but instead started to dismantle haystacks and load them onto the lorries. However, with an angry crowd gathering in the lane behind them, they soon reconsidered and drove off.

To continue the walk, enter the field at the finger-post and keep ahead across the field, soon converging with a small stream. Walk along the bank of the stream.

Look back to see Elmsett Hall Farm on the skyline.

Follow the stream to the far corner of the field and turn right, following the field boundary to reach a lane.

❸   **For the shorter route**: Cross the lane and take a footpath leading off to the right side of the lane, opposite the gate to Red House Farm. Follow a footpath across the middle of a field, aiming for the right end of trees seen on the skyline. On the far side of the field, turn left for 100 yards, then turn right along the edge of the wood. At the end of the wood maintain the same direction along the edge of a field. Go through a gap in the hedge at the end of the field and maintain your direction, aiming at the middle of a row of houses on the opposite side of the field. Keep ahead to rejoin the longer route at Point 5 below.

For the longer route: Turn left and follow the quiet country lane for

¾ mile. Pass a side road to Somersham and keep ahead for a further 200 yards to reach Rhoods Farm. Walk past the farm for 50 yards. At the end of the farm buildings turn right and follow an overgrown footpath, initially down the side of the farm and then continuing along the hedgerow. Go right then left with the hedge, then keep ahead on a broad path down the field. At the bottom of the slope cross a culvert and immediately turn right onto a footpath along the edge of a field.

❹ Follow the footpath along the side of the field and through a small wood. Cross a tarmac drive and keep straight on along the edge of a field. At a 'headland' of the field keep ahead on a defined path to reach the hedge opposite. Continue ahead, the hedge on your right. Just after the hedge on your right ends, turn right across a plank bridge and immediately turn left. Continue in your former direction, now on the left-hand side of a field. Cross a dirt track at the end of the field and keep straight on along a clear path across the next field. On the far side of the field go through a waymarked gap in the hedge, then keep straight on across the next field, aiming just to the right of buildings opposite. At the far side of the field turn left.

❺ (**The shorter route rejoins here.**) Follow a green path between a fence and hedge to reach a lane. Turn right and follow the lane to a T-junction. Turn left back to the start.

The victory of the people of Elmsett on 2nd May 1932 was a temporary one, and bailiffs for the Church returned to seize livestock and further hay belonging to Charles Westren, valued at some £1,200. This was then put up for auction in nearby Sudbury but, as no local people would bid for impounded produce, the Church could find few buyers. It had failed to recover its last rent, and bankrupted Charles Westren in the process. For the next four years cases such as this occurred across much of Suffolk, losing the Church any popular support it may have had. The press dubbed these events the 'Tithe Wars'. In 1936 the law was changed, and farmers received exemption from paying the tithe rent, although it was not officially abolished until 1977.

WALK 16
SHEPHERDS GROVE AND THE WAR IN THE AIR 1943–45

Length: 4 miles

One of the perfectly preserved observation towers built in 1943 and still standing at Shepherds Grove

HOW TO GET THERE: Walsham Le Willows is 4 miles east of Ixforth, on a minor road clearly signposted off the A143. The walk starts from the village church.

PARKING: There is ample roadside parking in the village, but please park with consideration for residents.

MAP: OS Landranger 155 (GR 000712).

INTRODUCTION

This gentle walk starts in the attractive village of Walsham Le Willows, and then uses footpaths and a few quiet lanes. It follows field and woodland paths, pausing to explore the remains of RAF Shepherds Grove. The terrain is flat and easy underfoot.

THE HISTORICAL BACKGROUND

When one walks around the tranquil countryside of rural Suffolk today, it is hard to imagine that during the Second World War this county was in the front line, but the ghosts of that conflict can be felt at Shepherds Grove airfield.

During the dark days of 1940 and 1941, England stood alone against Nazi Germany, facing a future that looked bleak in the extreme. The military situation improved tremendously with the entry of the USA into the war in 1941. The immediate impact of this was the stationing of the American Eighth Air Force (USAAF) in Britain. This was an enormous body of men and machines, which, by the time its transfer to England was completed, was twice the size of the RAF.

A total of 75 new airfields were needed to accommodate the USAAF, predominantly in East Anglia, the most convenient launch pad for bombing raids into Germany. Work started on Shepherds Grove airfield in 1943, but before it was completed in early 1944 it had become superfluous to US requirements. Instead, it was allocated to the RAF, and used to station 196th Squadron of Group Transport Command. This Group, using mainly Stirling and Halifax two-engined bombers, had the difficult task of flying supplies to soldiers operating behind enemy lines.

The SOE (Special Operations Executive) had been formed to infiltrate resistance fighters into occupied Europe and keep them supplied. After Allied troops landed in France in June 1944, the scale of resistance operations increased dramatically. Throughout the following winter 196 Squadron flew many sorties over Holland, Denmark and Norway, parachuting arms and supplies to the Resistance. As the war moved closer to the German border, the squadron was engaged in dropping units of the newly formed SAS, Britain's elite commando force, behind enemy lines to prepare the way for the forthcoming invasion. In March 1945, 196 Squadron took part in the invasion of Germany, towing gliders full of troops across the Rhine to seize bridges and strategic towns. Although the

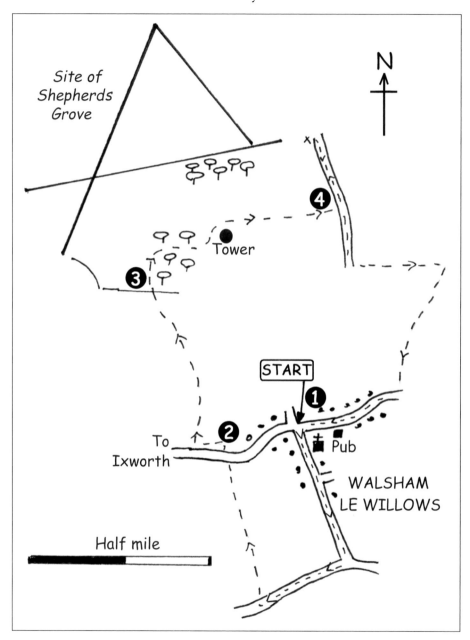

war was obviously coming to a conclusion, 196 Squadron continued to fly low-level sorties over occupied Holland and Norway, supplying the Resistance and the SAS.

The RAF continued to use Shepherd Grove as an airfield until 1950, when it was transferred to the USAAF as a base against a perceived new enemy (Russia). In 1951 a squadron of American Sabre jets was sent to Shepherds Grove, the first foreign aircraft to be assigned to defend Britain in the Cold War. The USAAF operated out of Shepherd Grove until 1958, when they transferred their operations to nearby Lakenheath. Shepherds Grove, abandoned, fell beneath the plough and was largely forgotten.

THE WALK

❶   Standing at the crossroads in Walsham Le Willows, with the Six Bells behind you and the church on your left, walk downhill (signed 'Badwell Heath').

The church of St Mary dates from the late 13th century, and is well worth a visit when open. In particular, it has a wonderful hammer-beamed oak roof, decorated with wooden suns, the badge of both King Edward IV and his brother-in-law the Duke of Suffolk, whose manor this was. Behind the altar is a spectacular terracotta reredos, a decorative panel displaying the Last Supper, carved in 1883.

Cross Grange Road and keep straight on. At a T-junction, turn right, still signed 'Badwell Heath'. Continue along the road for ¼ mile. Some 200 yards past the de-restricted speed signs, turn right at a finger-post through the hedge and into a field. Keep ahead along the side of a field, with the hedge close on your right. At the end of the field go through a kissing gate and cross the lane to a metal squeeze stile on the far side.

❷   Go through the stile and immediately turn left along a footpath. In 150 yards turn right over a footbridge. Go through a metal squeeze stile in front of you and keep ahead along an enclosed footpath. Follow the footpath as it winds through scrubland to reach a field. Keep ahead along the side of the field, with the hedge close on your right, to reach a concrete drive.

This concrete track is the remains of the perimeter road that encircled RAF Shepherds Grove in 1943. With the arrival of the USAAF there was an

American Sabre Jets were stationed at RAF Shepherds Grove to defend Britain in the Cold War

urgent need to create many new airfields as quickly as possible, and thus they were built to a standard design, known as the 'Class A Bomber'. There was one main runway, built in the direction of the prevailing wind (east-west in the case of most Suffolk airfields). Two other interconnecting runways were built, to create an 'A' shape. A perimeter road ran around the outside of the 'A', connecting the runways to several hardstanding areas on which could be parked up to 36 bombers. Numerous buildings, for administration, maintenance, storage, etc., were dispersed around the field, all connected by the perimeter road and spurs leading off from it.

❸   Cross the drive and keep ahead on a footpath into woods. At a T-junction of footpaths, turn right. Soon turn left with the path, following it as it winds along the edge of the wood, to eventually emerge at a cross track.

Some 20 yards along the track leading to the right, in the trees on the left-hand side of the track, is an observation tower, built in 1943 and perfectly preserved. Several such towers remain along the line of an embankment, which in 1943 was the boundary between the airfield and the maintenance/administration area.

Bear slightly left into a field, then resume your previous direction, with the hedge now on your right.

You are walking parallel to the runways of the airfield, which were across the field to your left, behind the stand of trees. The grassy sward you are walking along provided parking for some of the 36 bombers stationed at RAF Shepherds Grove. Behind the hedge and embankment on your right were the workshops and technical stores. There were also two huge hangars, 120 feet wide and 39 feet high, where repairs on the huge bombers could be carried out. There are several small woods dotted around you. The airfield was built around and between these, to somewhat camouflage its profile from enemy aircraft. A mile behind you, not visible from this walk, is the small wood called Shepherds Grove, which gave its name to the airfield.

At a large gap in the hedge on your right, pause and look around.

Look first to your left, across the field. The main runway of RAF Shepherds Grove (which you can see in a short while) ran along the opposite side of the woods you can see. One of the two shorter runways ran from the corner of the wood, away from you – you are looking directly along its line. Now look behind you and to the right. Two observation towers can be seen along the line of the embankment that surrounded the maintenance area. The hangars stood on the open ground in front of you. The perimeter road you crossed earlier came over this ground, stretching for 3 miles around the whole airfield.

Continue with the hedge on your right to reach a road.

❹   To see the main runway, turn left along the road for 200 yards, to a concrete barrier blocking a gateway on the left.

The runway was directly ahead, and can still be clearly seen today as a concrete track. One of the secondary runways ran half right, in front of the trees ahead and to your right. The main runway was 2,000 yards long and 50 yards wide, the two subsidiary runways each about 1,400 yards long. By 1943 all runways were made of concrete, the grass runways made famous in Battle of Britain movies having been dispensed with. At the far end of the main runway was one of two huge underground fuel tanks, capable of holding 100,000 gallons of aviation fuel. Ammunition stores were also located at the far ends of the runways. Both fuel and explosives were stored as far as possible from the maintenance and administration area.

To continue the walk, return to where you joined the road and carry on along the road for 300 yards, then turn left onto an enclosed track at a finger-post. Follow the green track between hedges for ¼ mile, and then turn right at a finger-post to follow a green track across the middle of a large field. Keep ahead, a hedge eventually on your left, crossing a cross track and keeping ahead towards houses.

Hardcore can be seen in places along this track, another leftover from RAF Shepherds Grove. Domestic buildings to house the personnel from the base, a dozen or so men per hut, were spread across the surrounding countryside, to lessen the danger from enemy air attacks. This track led between the base and Walsham Le Willows, where many personnel, especially officers, were billeted.

As you approach the houses, zig-zag left then right again with the track. Follow the track past the front of bungalows to reach a road. Turn right and follow the road through the village.

Today Walsham Le Willows has a population of only 1,200, and despite improvements to the roads, is still relatively isolated. In 1943 it was a sleepy farming community, its population was smaller, and it was tucked away in the heart of the countryside, with only narrow country lanes to connect it to the outside world. The impact of building RAF Shepherds Grove a mere mile away, and the arrival of nearly 3,000 servicemen, must have turned the villagers' world upside down.

Follow the road to return to the Blue Boar and the church.